THE WORLD BLIND UNION GUIDE
TO THE MARRAKESH TREATY

More Praise for
The World Blind Union Guide to the Marrakesh Treaty

"This Guide to the Marrakesh Treaty, written by world-renowned copyright scholars, is essential for anyone who aims to transpose, interpret, and apply the norms in the Treaty in an effective manner, finally giving visually impaired people real access to knowledge and culture."

Lucie Guibault
Institute for Information Law
University of Amsterdam

"This book provides a timely, clear, and insightful guide to a complex and novel legal subject with immense practical significance. A must-read for anybody interested in making accessible versions of printed material available to disabled people."

Anna Lawson
Professor of Law and Director of the
Centre for Disability Studies
University of Leeds

THE WORLD BLIND UNION GUIDE TO THE MARRAKESH TREATY

Facilitating Access to Books for
Print-Disabled Individuals

Laurence R. Helfer

Molly K. Land

Ruth L. Okediji

Jerome H. Reichman

UNIVERSITY PRESS

Oxford University Press is a department of the University of Oxford. It furthers the University's objective of excellence in research, scholarship, and education by publishing worldwide. Oxford is a registered trademark of Oxford University Press in the UK and certain other countries.

Published in the United States of America by Oxford University Press
198 Madison Avenue, New York, NY 10016, United States of America.

© Oxford University Press 2017

All rights reserved. No part of this publication may be reproduced, stored in a retrieval system, or transmitted, in any form or by any means, without the prior permission in writing of Oxford University Press, or as expressly permitted by law, by license, or under terms agreed with the appropriate reproduction rights organization. Inquiries concerning reproduction outside the scope of the above should be sent to the Rights Department, Oxford University Press, at the address above.

You must not circulate this work in any other form
and you must impose this same condition on any acquirer.

Library of Congress Cataloging-in-Publication Data

Names: Helfer, Laurence R., author. | World Blind Union.
Title: The World Blind Union guide to the Marrakesh Treaty : facilitating
   access to books for print-disabled individuals / Laurence R. Helfer, Molly K. Land,
   Ruth L. Okediji, Jerome H. Reichman.
Other titles: Guide to the Marrakesh Treaty
Description: New York : Oxford University Press, 2017. | Includes bibliographical
   references and index.
Identifiers: LCCN 2016050772| ISBN 9780190679644 ((hardback) : alk. paper) |
   ISBN 9780190679651 ((pbk.) : alk. paper)
Subjects: LCSH: Marrakesh Treaty to Facilitate Access to Published Works for Persons who are
   Blind, Visually Impaired, or Otherwise Print Disabled (2013 June 27) |
   People with visual disabilities—Services for. | People with visual disabilities—
   Means of communication. | Intellectual property. | Human rights.
Classification: LCC K637.A42013 W67 2017 | DDC 342.08/7—dc23 LC record available at
https://lccn.loc.gov/2016050772

---

1 3 5 7 9 8 6 4 2

Paperback printed by Webcom, Inc., Canada
Hardback printed by Bridgeport National Bindery, Inc., United States of America

Note to Readers

This publication is designed to provide accurate and authoritative information in regard to the subject matter covered. It is based upon sources believed to be accurate and reliable and is intended to be current as of the time it was written. It is sold with the understanding that the publisher is not engaged in rendering legal, accounting, or other professional services. If legal advice or other expert assistance is required, the services of a competent professional person should be sought. Also, to confirm that the information has not been affected or changed by recent developments, traditional legal research techniques should be used, including checking primary sources where appropriate.

*(Based on the Declaration of Principles jointly adopted by a Committee of the
American Bar Association and a Committee of Publishers and Associations.)*

**You may order this or any other Oxford University Press publication
by visiting the Oxford University Press website at www.oup.com.**

The Marrakesh Treaty to Facilitate Access to Published Works for Persons Who Are Blind, Visually Impaired, or Otherwise Print Disabled

Opened for Signature: June 27, 2013
States Parties: 25 as of November 30, 2016
Entry into Force: September 30, 2016

CONTENTS

Acknowledgments   xiii
Foreword   xv
Executive Summary   xvii
Introduction   xxi

1. Guiding Principles for the Marrakesh Treaty   1
   1.1. The Marrakesh Treaty at the Crossroads of Human Rights and Intellectual Property   2
      1.1.1. The International Human Rights Regime   2
      1.1.2. The International Intellectual Property Regime   4
      1.1.3. Conflict or Coexistence between the Regimes?   5
      1.1.4. Using Copyright Tools to Achieve Human Rights Ends   8
   1.2. Interpretive Principles for the Marrakesh Treaty   11
      1.2.1. Emphasize Object and Purpose   11
      1.2.2. Adapt the Marrakesh Treaty to Changing Conditions   14

CONTENTS

1.2.3. Promote Consistency with the CRPD	15
1.2.3.1. Background to the CRPD	16
1.2.3.2. Central Principles of the CRPD	16
1.2.3.3. Consultations with Stakeholders	19
2. The Legal and Policy Choices in the Marrakesh Treaty	21
2.1. Copyrighted Works Covered by the Marrakesh Treaty	21
2.2. Accessible Format Copies	23
2.3. Authorized Entities	24
2.3.1. Introduction and Overview	24
2.3.2. Types of Authorized Entities	26
2.3.2.1. Entities Providing Services to Beneficiaries	27
2.3.2.2. Government Recognized Entities	29
2.3.3. The Practices of Authorized Entities	30
2.4. Beneficiary Persons	31
2.4.1. Introduction and Overview	31
2.4.2. Categories of Beneficiary Persons	32
2.4.2.1. Blindness	33
2.4.2.2. Visual Impairment or Perceptual Disability	33
2.4.2.3. Physical Reading Disability	35
2.4.3. Defining Beneficiary Persons in Implementing Legislation	36
2.5. Exceptions and Limitations to Copyright in National Law	38
2.5.1. Introduction and Overview	38
2.5.2. Obligations of Article 4(1)	41
2.5.2.1. Mandatory Exceptions and Limitations	41

2.5.2.2. Non-mandatory Exceptions and
Limitations   43
2.5.3. Modes of Implementing Article 4(1)   43
   2.5.3.1. Article 4(2)—The Safe Harbor
   Option   43
      2.5.3.1.1. The Safe Harbor for
      Authorized Entities   44
      2.5.3.1.2. The Safe Harbor for
      Beneficiary Persons   45
      2.5.3.1.3. Implications of the Safe
      Harbor Options   45
   2.5.3.2. Article 4(3)—The Sui Generis
   Option   46
2.5.4. Exceptions and Limitations for the
Translation of Copyrighted Works   47
2.5.5. The Commercial Availability Option   47
2.5.6. The Remuneration Option   49
2.6. Cross-Border Exchange and Importation of
Accessible Format Copies   51
   2.6.1. Introduction and Overview   51
   2.6.2. Substantive Obligations of Articles 5 and 6   53
      2.6.2.1. Article 5—Export of Accessible
      Format Copies   53
      2.6.2.2. Article 6—Import of Accessible
      Format Copies   55
   2.6.3. Modes of Implementation of Articles 5
   and 6   56
      2.6.3.1. Article 5(2)—The Safe Harbor
      Option   56
      2.6.3.2. Article 5(3)—The Sui Generis
      Option   57

CONTENTS

    2.6.4. Exhaustion of Rights   59
    2.6.5. Implementation of Article 6   60
    2.6.6. Cross-Border Issues Not Addressed in the
          Marrakesh Treaty   61
2.7. Technological Protection Measures   62
    2.7.1. Introduction and Overview   62
    2.7.2. Analysis   63
2.8. The Three-Step Test   67
    2.8.1. Policy Rationales of the Three-Step Test   68
    2.8.2. The Three-Step Test and Exceptions and
          Limitations for the Blind   69
    2.8.3. Applying the Three-Step Test to the
          Marrakesh Treaty   70
    2.8.4. The Three-Step Test and International
          Human Rights Law   73

3. Putting the Marrakesh Treaty into Practice in
National Law   75
  3.1. Create Legal Remedies   76
  3.2. Empower National Institutions   78
    3.2.1. Human Rights Institutions   78
    3.2.2. Intellectual Property Institutions   80
    3.2.3. Linking to the Marrakesh Treaty
          Assembly   81
  3.3. Undertake Enforcement Activities   81
    3.3.1. Monitor Rights   82
    3.3.2. Enforce Legal Remedies   83
    3.3.3. Create a National Plan of Action   83
    3.3.4. Engage in Training and Outreach   85
  3.4. Engage in National Reporting   85
    3.4.1. UN Treaty Bodies   86

3.4.2. UN Charter Bodies	88
3.4.3. UN Special Procedures	89
Conclusion	91

Appendices

1: World Intellectual Property Organization, Extraordinary General Assembly: A Decision Text (December 18, 2012)	93
2: Marrakesh Treaty to Facilitate Access to Published Works for Persons Who Are Blind, Visually Impaired, or Otherwise Print Disabled (adopted on June 27, 2013, entered into force on September 30, 2016)	95
3: Signatories and Contracting Parties to the Marrakesh Treaty (as of October 31, 2016)	109
4: Convention on the Rights of Persons with Disabilities and Optional Protocol (adopted on December 13, 2006, entered into force on May 3, 2008)	115
5: Signatories and Contracting Parties to the Convention on the Rights of Persons with Disabilities (as of October 31, 2016)	150
6: Berne Convention for the Protection of Literary and Artistic Works (Paris Text, as last amended on September 28, 1979)	159
Index	205

ACKNOWLEDGMENTS

The World Blind Union and the authors of *The World Blind Union Guide to the Marrakesh Treaty: Facilitating Access to Books for Print-Disabled Individuals* acknowledge with deep appreciation the contributions of former Treaty negotiators, human rights advocates, nongovernmental organizations, and scholars and practitioners in copyright law, human rights law, and disability law, whose helpful comments and suggestions greatly contributed to the completion of this Guide.

Experts' workshops were held on November 6–7, 2015 at Harvard Law School and on January 28–29, 2016 at the University of Amsterdam's Institute for Information Law. The workshops focused on understanding the provisions of the Treaty from the perspectives of copyright law, human rights law, and disability law, as well as the technological issues related to the creation, access, and use of accessible format copies. The workshop discussions were significantly enriched by the insights of three negotiators of the Treaty and other experts present at WIPO in Geneva and at the Diplomatic Conference in Marrakesh.

The authors are especially grateful to the following individuals for their feedback on earlier drafts of the Guide: Jonathan Band, Maryanne Diamond, Séverine Dusollier, Jim Fruchterman, G. Anthony Giannoumis, Henning Grosse Ruse-Kahn, Lucie Guibault, Teresa Hackett, Stuart Hamilton, Peter Jaszi, Koen Krikhaar, Anna Lawson, Jonathan Lazar,

ACKNOWLEDGMENTS

Kenneth Félix Haczynski da Nóbrega, Dan Pescod, Gudibende Raghavender, Jerome Reichman, Martin Senftleben, Lea Shaver, Michael Stein, and Paul Torremans. We are also grateful to the International Federation of Library Associations and Institutions (IFLA) and the Electronic Information for Libraries (EIFL) for their comments and input on the Guide.

Finally, the World Blind Union expresses its sincere appreciation to the following organizations: the Open Society Foundations (OSF), which provided significant financial support for Phase 1 and Phase 2 of the Marrakesh Ratification and Implementation Campaign, of which this Guide is a key component; CBM; Sightsavers; Royal National Institute of Blind Persons (RNIB); Vision Australia; International Council for Education of People with Visual Impairment (ICEVI); and the National Federation of the Blind India.

FOREWORD

The Marrakesh Treaty to Facilitate Access to Published Works for Persons Who Are Blind, Visually Impaired, or Otherwise Print Disabled marks a breakthrough in enabling the blind and other print-handicapped persons to access the printed word. Ensuring that visually impaired persons have sustainable access to published works on the same terms as sighted persons is an important milestone toward realizing the vision of a world in which all persons can participate fully and equally in the political, economic, and cultural life of society.

In about one-third of the world's nations, exceptions to local copyright laws have long assisted blind persons such as me in obtaining books and other materials in accessible formats, such as Braille and audio recordings. Even where these exceptions existed, however, books in accessible formats could not cross international borders. In Spain, for example, there are approximately 100,000 accessible books, whereas Argentina has only about 25,000. Yet Spain's accessible books cannot be exported legally to Argentina or to other Spanish-speaking countries. The Marrakesh Treaty (MT) enables accessible format copies to cross borders where the exporting and importing countries both have appropriate copyright exceptions. The MT not only facilitates these cross-border exchanges, it also prescribes a framework for harmonizing copyright exceptions to benefit all print-handicapped persons.

FOREWORD

Like most treaties, the MT contains a number of complex provisions. This Guide skillfully unpacks these provisions to make the Treaty comprehensible to parliamentarians and publishers, as well as to persons with disabilities and to our representative organisations.

The Guide is divided into three parts. The first part explains why the MT should be broadly interpreted because it brings about a convergence between intellectual property treaties and human rights covenants and conventions—and especially the Convention on the Rights of Persons with Disabilities (CRPD). In the middle part, the nuts and bolts of the MT are explained to assist ratifying countries in enacting national implementing legislation. The final part discusses how to put the Marrakesh Treaty into practice, including making the MT and its implementing legislation part of each country's national disability action plan.

As a former member and past chair of the United Nations Committee on the Rights of Persons with Disabilities, I am especially pleased that the authors of this Guide have provided a useful and highly accessible resource for those seeking to understand and give effect to the Marrakesh Treaty. The Committee has been urging countries to speedily ratify the Marrakesh Treaty as a means of making the printed word accessible, thus fulfilling one of the major aims of the CRPD. I hope that when fully implemented with the aid of this Guide, the MT will increase the very small percentage of works available in accessible formats and help to equalize what remains a very uneven playing field.

Ron McCallum AO
Emeritus Professor and Former Dean of the
University of Sydney Law School
Past Chair, United Nations Committee on the
Rights of Persons with Disabilities
Sydney, Australia
30 November 2016

EXECUTIVE SUMMARY

The Marrakesh Treaty to Facilitate Access to Published Works for Persons Who Are Blind, Visually Impaired, or Otherwise Print Disabled (Marrakesh Treaty, MT, or Treaty) is an international agreement negotiated under the auspices of the World Intellectual Property Organization (WIPO) and adopted at a diplomatic conference in Marrakesh, Morocco, in June 2013. The overarching objective of the MT is to expand the availability of copyrighted works to the nearly 300 million individuals with print disabilities around the world. Many of these individuals—who include not only those who are blind or visually impaired but also persons with physical reading or perceptual disabilities—currently lack adequate access to books and other cultural materials in accessible formats.

The Marrakesh Treaty has enjoyed strong support from countries around the world. Fifty-one countries signed the MT at the conclusion of the diplomatic conference in Marrakesh in June 2013; as of July 2016, more than 75 countries have signed the Treaty. The MT entered into force on September 30, 2016, three months after 20 states had ratified the Treaty.*

---

* The first twenty countries to ratify the MT were: Argentina, Australia, Brazil, Canada, Chile, Democratic People's Republic of Korea, Ecuador, El Salvador, Guatemala, India, Israel, Mali, Mexico, Mongolia, Paraguay, Peru, Republic of Korea, Singapore, United Arab Emirates, and Uruguay.

EXECUTIVE SUMMARY

Governments in ratifying countries will face a variety of legal and policy choices as they decide how to incorporate the MT into their national legal systems. These choices will determine whether the Treaty realizes its overarching objective—to enhance the human rights of print-disabled persons by facilitating their ability to create, read, and share books and other cultural materials in accessible formats.

The World Blind Union Guide to the Marrakesh Treaty: Facilitating Access to Books for Print-Disabled Individuals provides a comprehensive analysis of the MT to help countries to achieve this goal. The Guide is intended for multiple audiences, including:

- parliamentarians and policymakers, who adopt domestic legislation and regulations to give effect to the Treaty;
- judges and administrators, who interpret and apply those laws;
- disability rights organizations and other civil society groups, who advocate for the Treaty's implementation and effective enforcement;
- international and national monitoring and oversight bodies, who review government implementation and enforcement measures; and
- print-disabled individuals, who are the MT's explicitly identified "beneficiary persons."

To assist these actors and other stakeholders, the Guide offers a general conceptual framework for interpreting and implementing the Marrakesh Treaty, an article-by-article analysis of the Treaty's key provisions, and specific legal and policy recommendations for giving effect to these provisions. The Guide is intended to be read either as a whole or selectively. For readers who wish to focus on specific topics, the Guide is written in such a way that each section should stand on its own without the need for additional background reading.

In terms of its conceptual approach, the Guide views the MT as an international agreement that employs the legal doctrines and policy tools of copyright law to advance human rights ends. This approach is inspired

EXECUTIVE SUMMARY

by several features of the Treaty, including its express references to widely-adopted international human rights instruments in the first paragraph of the Preamble, its status as the first multilateral agreement to establish mandatory exceptions to the exclusive rights of copyright owners, and its designation of print-disabled individuals as the Treaty's beneficiaries. At the same time, the Guide recognizes that states have obligations under international intellectual property law as well as international human rights law. These preexisting commitments—which include the three-step test for constraining exceptions to copyright that is found in several intellectual property treaties—must also be respected by governments in deciding how best to give effect to the MT.

The Guide explains the legal and policy options that the Marrakesh Treaty provides to ratifying countries, and it offers recommendations for choosing among the available options in light of states' preexisting human rights and copyright commitments. For example, the Guide urges states to enact mandatory exceptions to copyright that the Treaty designates as presumptively compatible with existing intellectual property treaties. These "safe harbor" provisions include exceptions to the exclusive rights of reproduction, distribution, making available to the public, and public performance (Article 4), and exceptions for cross-border transfers of accessible format copies (Article 5). For ratifying countries that choose a different approach, such as general fair use or fair dealing exceptions, the Guide offers a number of recommendations to assist governments in tailoring implementing legislation to their domestic policy goals and the needs of print-disabled persons.

The Guide also adopts a position on MT clauses that are permissive rather than mandatory. The two most important of these optional provisions are the commercial availability requirement in Article 4(4) and the remuneration requirement in Article 4(5). The first clause permits a country to ban the creation of accessible format copies if the copyright owner has already made the work commercially available in that particular format. The second clause permits a state to require compensation as a condition of creating or distributing accessible format copies. The Guide considers these optional provisions to be in tension with the MT's overarching objectives. Accordingly, the Guide urges states to eschew these optional measures.

EXECUTIVE SUMMARY

In its final part, the Guide addresses the implementation of the Marrakesh Treaty. Giving domestic effect to the MT is not a difficult, complex, or expensive endeavor. At the most basic level, each ratifying country must revise its national copyright laws to authorize the making, using, and sharing of accessible format copies, including sharing across borders.

As with any treaty, changes to national law alone may not ensure effective realization of the MT's objectives. The Guide thus recommends that states build on their existing implementation of human rights treaties by taking a range of concrete steps to monitor and enforce the MT. In particular, officials should consult with print-disabled individuals and their representative organizations, create effective legal procedures to remedy violations, empower national human rights and intellectual property institutions to oversee implementation of the Treaty, and report on implementation measures to the United Nations. The institutions and administrative mechanisms for carrying out these activities already exist in most national legal systems or can be easily adapted to include the implementation of the MT.

INTRODUCTION

The Marrakesh Treaty to Facilitate Access to Published Works for Persons Who Are Blind, Visually Impaired, or Otherwise Print Disabled (the Marrakesh Treaty, MT, or Treaty) creates mandatory exceptions to copyright for the benefit of individuals with print disabilities. The rights in the MT that flow from these exceptions share a common overarching aim: to facilitate the ability of these individuals to make, consume, and share copyrighted works in accessible formats.

The Marrakesh Treaty was negotiated against the backdrop of a worldwide paucity of printed works and cultural materials in accessible formats—often referred to as a "book famine." This global famine is alarming in its scope and impact. Many of the estimated 300 million print-disabled persons around the world, especially those living in developing countries, lack adequate access to printed materials in accessible formats even though the technology to create such works has long existed and continues to evolve rapidly. Unable to read newspapers, enjoy books, or research on the Internet, these individuals cannot participate meaningfully in society. The result is a violation of numerous internationally recognized human rights, including, most notably, the rights protected by the Convention on the Rights of Persons with Disabilities (CRPD). Adopted by 168 countries as of October 2016—more than 85 percent of the United Nations membership—the CRPD requires governments to ensure that intellectual property laws do not prevent disabled persons from accessing books and other cultural materials.

Collective action to end the book famine required a forceful multilateral response in the form of a new treaty to harmonize exceptions to copyright to benefit print-disabled individuals. A legally binding international agreement was needed for several reasons. First, the scarcity of copyrighted works in accessible formats is a global problem that requires a global solution. All national laws limit copyright protection to achieve important public policy goals, and exceptions for the blind are among the most long-standing of these limitations. Nonetheless, more than two-thirds of countries have not adopted such exceptions. In addition, many of the exceptions that exist do not fully satisfy the needs of print-disabled persons, especially in developing nations and with respect to new technologies such as e-books and audiobooks.

Second, because copyright laws are territorial in scope, many existing national exceptions do not permit the import or export of accessible format copies. It is neither desirable nor efficient for every country to provide all of the accessible format copies needed to end the book famine in its territory, especially if such copies are readily available elsewhere. Thus, a principal goal of the MT is to require states to adopt copyright exceptions that facilitate the exchange of accessible format copies across borders.

Third, most of the world's nations are already required to facilitate access by disabled persons to copyrighted works, either by the human rights treaties they have joined or by their own domestic legislation. The most concrete example of this legal commitment appears in the widely-ratified CRPD, mentioned above. The MT provides a template for countries to satisfy these preexisting international obligations, including by building on steps they have already taken to give effect to the CRPD and other human rights treaties.

Inspired by these multiple rationales for global collective action, this Guide provides a roadmap for interpreting and implementing the Marrakesh Treaty. The World Blind Union hopes to assist government officials, policymakers, disability rights organizations, and civil society groups who will decide how to give effect to the MT in ratifying countries.

The Guide identifies the legal and policy choices available to these actors, and it offers recommendations that advance the Treaty's foundational objective—to use mandatory exceptions to copyright protection to expand the availability of accessible format books and cultural materials to print-disabled individuals.

As the first international agreement to require exceptions to copyright to enhance the human rights of a specific population, the Marrakesh Treaty lies at the intersection of international human rights law and international intellectual property law. In interpreting and implementing the MT, therefore, public officials and private actors must strive to comply with both sets of legal obligations.

But how can governments achieve this consistency? The Guide offers a practical answer. It conceives of the Marrakesh Treaty as an international instrument that employs the legal doctrines and policy tools of copyright to achieve human rights objectives. This vision of the Treaty underpins the analysis in the Guide. It informs the general interpretive principles described in Chapter 1, the article-by-article analysis and policy options discussed in Chapter 2, and the recommendations for implementing the MT in domestic law reviewed in Chapter 3.

This framing of the Marrakesh Treaty as a multilateral agreement that uses intellectual property means to achieve human rights ends has a number of general implications. First, it requires governments to ensure that their implementation of the MT is effective. Treaty rights and obligations that exist on paper but not in reality are insufficient; they will not expand the availability of accessible format copies to print-disabled persons.

Second, the Guide's conceptual approach informs its recommendations about the policy options available to governments. The Marrakesh Treaty expressly refers to other copyright conventions and human rights instruments. The MT cannot be interpreted in isolation from these legal texts, including the three-step test for exceptions and limitations that appears in multiple intellectual property agreements. Nevertheless, by providing what this Guide labels as "safe harbor" exceptions for creating, using, and sharing accessible format copies, the MT affirms that the three-step test is flexible enough to coexist with states' ongoing commitments to protecting human rights.

Third, where states have discretion under the Treaty, the Guide recommends choices that promote rather than limit access. For example, the Guide urges states to reject optional clauses in the MT concerning remuneration and commercial availability. Although these provisions are formally compatible with the Treaty, their implementation could significantly limit the access of beneficiary persons, thus undermining the Treaty's object and purpose.

Finally, the MT does not restrict preexisting authority under domestic and international law to adopt exceptions and limitations to copyright that serve public interest goals. States may continue to rely on this authority to create, preserve, and extend such exceptions and limitations—including those that further the human rights of persons with disabilities—provided that doing so is compatible with the intellectual property agreements they have ratified. Thus, although the MT provides a model for protecting the rights of print-disabled individuals to access copyrighted works, the Treaty does not preclude states from going beyond its terms.

The remainder of this Guide proceeds as follows. Chapter 1 begins with a brief introduction to the intellectual property and human rights regimes. It then identifies three general principles of treaty interpretation that inform the Guide's analysis—emphasizing the MT's object and purpose, adapting the Treaty to changing conditions, and promoting consistency with the CRPD.

Chapter 2 consists of an article-by-article analysis of the MT's requirements. It describes the Treaty's basic structure and identifies the legal and policy choices available to governments for each of its key provisions—including the definitions of "accessible format copy," "authorized entities," and "beneficiary persons"—and the exceptions and limitations to copyright protection that all ratifying countries must adopt.

Chapter 3 of the Guide turns to implementation. The core obligation of ratifying states is to revise national copyright laws to authorize print-disabled individuals and authorized entities to make, consume, and share accessible format copies, including across borders. But as with any treaty, changes to the law may not be enough to ensure the MT's effectiveness.

INTRODUCTION

The Guide thus recommends that governments build on their preexisting implementation of human rights agreements by taking a range of concrete steps to monitor and enforce the MT. These steps include consulting with print-disabled individuals, creating legal procedures to remedy violations, empowering national institutions to monitor and enforce international commitments, and reporting on implementation measures within the United Nations' human rights system.

Chapter 1

Guiding Principles for the Marrakesh Treaty

The Marrakesh Treaty to Facilitate Access to Published Works for Persons Who Are Blind, Visually Impaired, or Otherwise Print Disabled (Marrakesh Treaty, MT, or Treaty) is an international agreement that seeks to eliminate the barriers that copyright law creates for print-disabled individuals in accessing books and other cultural materials. The MT achieves this objective by requiring states to adopt exceptions and limitations to copyright to enable the creation and distribution of accessible format copies, including across borders.

The Marrakesh Treaty seeks to advance human rights using the legal and policy tools of copyright. The very first lines of the MT's Preamble emphasize the overlap between these two legal fields, recalling "the principles of non-discrimination, equal opportunity, accessibility and full and effective participation and inclusion in society, proclaimed in the Universal Declaration of Human Rights and the United Nations Convention on the Rights of Persons with Disabilities" (CRPD), and recognizing "the need to maintain a balance between the effective protection of the rights of authors and the larger public interest." The MT thus helps to fulfill the promise made by contracting states in Article 30(3) of the CRPD "to ensure that laws protecting intellectual property rights do not constitute an unreasonable or discriminatory barrier to access by persons with disabilities to cultural materials."

The MT's distinctive blend of human rights and intellectual property means that the interpretation and implementation of the Treaty must take account of the legal obligations and principles of both fields. This Guide offers a comprehensive approach to these issues. It suggests policy options and practical considerations to promote the effective realization of the MT's objectives in a range of local settings. Before turning to these proposals, Section 1.1. of the Guide provides a brief introduction to the international human rights and intellectual property regimes, with an emphasis on copyright. Section 1.2 then explains how the human rights objectives that the MT seeks to achieve inform the interpretation of the Treaty under long-standing principles of public international law.

1.1. THE MARRAKESH TREATY AT THE CROSSROADS OF HUMAN RIGHTS AND INTELLECTUAL PROPERTY

The international human rights and international intellectual property (IP) regimes have expanded exponentially over the last two decades, leading to increased engagement between the two legal fields. Interpreting and implementing the MT will require careful consideration of the complementary and sometimes competing goals of each regime.

1.1.1. The International Human Rights Regime

The international system that protects the fundamental rights of all human beings arose following the Second World War. Confronted with clear evidence of mass atrocities, the victors of that conflict resolved that abuses perpetrated by a state against its own citizens and within its own borders would no longer be the concern of that state alone. The initial response to this commitment was to create the United Nations and vest it with responsibility for maintaining international peace and security and promoting universal respect for and observance of international human rights. Soon after its founding, the United Nations began the task of drafting the Universal Declaration of Human Rights (UDHR), a nonbinding resolution adopted unanimously by the UN General Assembly in 1948. During the decades that followed, the international human rights system focused on two principal tasks—expanding and refining a list of protected rights and freedoms, and creating international institutions and monitoring mechanisms to ensure that states respect those rights and freedoms in practice.

The core of international human rights law is contained in three legal instruments—the UDHR, the International Covenant on Civil and Political Rights (ICCPR), and the International Covenant on Economic, Social and Cultural Rights (ICESCR)—collectively known as the International Bill of Rights. The ICCPR and ICESCR, both adopted in 1966, translate the aspirational norms of the UDHR into legally binding obligations for states. The ICCPR protects a broad range of civil and political liberties, such as freedom of expression, freedom of thought, privacy, and the right to take part in the conduct of public affairs. The ICESCR protects the right to education, the right to participate in cultural life, and the right to enjoy the benefits of scientific progress and its applications, among other rights. Many of these rights are also incorporated in national constitutions, legislation, administrative regulations, and judicial decisions.

In addition to the ICCPR and the ICESCR, eight other UN treaties address specific human rights issues, including racial discrimination, torture, women's rights, children's rights, and disability rights. The treaty addressing the rights of individuals with disabilities is the Convention on the Rights of Persons with Disabilities (CRPD). Each of these UN treaties creates an international monitoring mechanism known as a "treaty body"—a committee of legal and other experts charged with overseeing that treaty's implementation and assessing whether states are complying with the rights that it protects. For the CRPD, these functions are performed by the Committee on the Rights of Persons with Disabilities (CRPD Committee). Article 39 of the CRPD gives the Committee the competence to, among other functions, "make suggestions and general recommendations based on the examination of reports and information received from the States Parties." Although the suggestions and recommendations of the CRPD Committee—referred to as General Comments—are not binding and cannot amend the CRPD, the interpretations generated by the Committee are entitled to "great weight" because of their unique role as independent expert bodies established to monitor state compliance with the treaties.[1]

1.1.2. The International Intellectual Property Regime

The 1967 Convention Establishing the World Intellectual Property Organization (WIPO) defines "intellectual property" as rights relating to "literary, artistic and scientific works; performances of performing artists, phonograms and broadcasts; inventions in all fields of human endeavor; scientific discoveries; industrial designs; trademarks, service marks, and commercial names and designations; protection against unfair competition; and all other rights resulting from intellectual activity in the industrial, scientific, literary or artistic fields."

This subsection focuses on copyright, which protects original works of authorship, such as the literary and artistic works that are the subject of the MT. A copyright exists as soon as a work of authorship, whether published or unpublished, is expressed in a tangible form. However, copyright protects only the form in which original ideas are expressed; the ideas themselves may be freely used by others. The owner of a copyrighted work has the exclusive right to, among other things, reproduce the work, prepare adaptations of the work (including translations), and distribute copies of the work. In addition to these economic rights, some countries also protect moral rights, including the rights to be named as the author and to object to derogatory treatment of a work.

The international rules protecting copyright have expanded significantly over the last century. Early bilateral and regional copyright treaties required states to grant foreign nationals the protections provided to their own nationals and established minimum standards of protection. These agreements focused on protecting the exclusive rights of creators

---

1. As the International Court of Justice recently explained regarding another treaty body, the UN Human Rights Committee, "[a]lthough the Court is in no way obliged ... to model its own interpretation ... on that of the Committee, it believes that it should ascribe great weight to the interpretation adopted by this independent body that was established specifically to supervise the application of that treaty." *Ahmadou Sadio Diallo (Republic of Guinea v. Democratic Republic of the Congo)*, Judgment, 2010 ICJ Rep. 639, 664.

and copyright owners, leaving states to regulate limitations and exceptions to those rights through domestic legislation. At the end of the nineteenth century, these principles were incorporated into a multilateral convention—the Berne Convention for the Protection of Literary and Artistic Works—which was revised and broadened over the next century to expand the protection of copyrighted works and regulate national exceptions and limitations. The administration of the Berne Convention was later entrusted to the WIPO.

In 1994, intellectual property (IP) was added to the mandate of the World Trade Organization (WTO) through the adoption of the Agreement on Trade-Related Aspects of Intellectual Property (TRIPS Agreement). The TRIPS Agreement enhanced the substantive protections of preexisting IP treaties—including the Berne Convention—and constrained states' authority to enact domestic limitations and exceptions. These heightened protections are mandatory for the entire WTO membership. The TRIPS Agreement also required WTO members to expand the mechanisms for the domestic enforcement of IP rights. Disputes over the interpretation and application of the treaty are adjudicated by the WTO Dispute Settlement Body, which can authorize trade sanctions against WTO members.

1.1.3. *Conflict or Coexistence between the Regimes?*

The simultaneous expansion of IP law and human rights law has increased the intersection between the two regimes, leading previously unrelated rules and institutions to interact in new and sometimes contested ways. Initially, some actors in the UN human rights system identified a direct conflict between the two regimes. These actors viewed expansive IP protections, such as those in the TRIPS Agreement, as making it more difficult for states to comply with human rights treaties.[2] For example, copyright provides exclusive rights that prevent third parties from reproducing or distributing protected works. If a copyright owner is unwilling or unable to make the work available in an accessible format, persons with

---

2. *Statement on Human Rights and Intellectual Property*, U.N. ESCOR Comm. on Econ., Soc., & Cultural Rts., 27th Sess., Agenda Item 3, para. 12, U.N. Doc. E/C.12/2001/15 (2001).

print disabilities cannot access that work. Without an applicable exception, the result is a restriction of these individuals' rights to freedom of expression, education, and cultural participation.

To resolve these conflicts, human rights experts urged states to recognize the primacy of human rights over IP laws and treaties on the ground that human rights are more fundamental. Advocates of this "conflicts approach" encouraged states to disregard or modify IP rules if necessary to comply with international human rights obligations. These advocates also highlighted conflicts to support the call to reform IP laws in ways that enhanced the protection of human rights, reframing demands for access to copyrighted works as internationally mandated entitlements that are equivalent or even superior to the economic rights of IP owners.

The conflicts approach usefully focused on the human rights consequences of IP and the importance of ensuring access to copyrighted works—issues that the IP regime had neglected. At the same time, however, the conflicts approach neglected the ways in which individual innovation and creativity—goals pursued by the IP system—are also essential to the fulfillment of human rights. Scholars, policymakers, and NGOs thus began to envision the human rights and IP regimes as asking the same basic question—how to give authors and inventors sufficient incentives to create and innovate while providing the public with adequate access to the products of their intellectual efforts. This has been called the coexistence approach.

This coexistence approach sees the two regimes as congruent rather than in conflict. Proponents of this approach accept the essential compatibility of the two regimes, while recognizing that they are sometimes in tension over how to strike the balance between incentives on the one hand and access on the other. For example, copyright provides an incentive for the creation of literary and artistic works by granting authors exclusive economic rights. Article 15 of the ICESCR recognizes a similar idea. It states that everyone has the right "[t]o benefit from the protection of the moral and material interests resulting from any scientific, literary or artistic production of which he [or she] is the author." Although human rights law does not protect IP as such,[3] it does protect the creative activities of

---

3. Intellectual property rights are protected under the right of property guaranteed in Article 1 of Protocol No. 1 to the European Convention on Human Rights. *Anheuser-Busch v. Portugal,*

individuals, including the economic interests of authors in achieving an adequate standard of living and their moral interests in maintaining the integrity of their works. Within both the IP and human rights regimes, therefore, IP is a means rather than an end; it is a mechanism to foster creativity and innovation and thereby contribute to the greater social good.

Both copyright law and human rights law also emphasize the importance of ensuring access to the products of creators' efforts. Article 15 of the ICESCR balances the protection of authors with the right of everyone "[t]o enjoy the benefits of scientific progress and its applications." Article 7 of the TRIPS Agreement identifies the treaty's objectives as contributing to innovation and technology transfer "to the mutual advantage of producers and users of technological knowledge and in a manner conducive to social and economic welfare, and to a balance of rights and obligations," whereas Article 8 recognizes the ability of states to take measures consistent with the treaty to promote the public interest. National laws include exceptions and limitations to copyright to achieve such interests. Common examples include copying by archives and libraries, limited quotations for purposes of commentary and criticism, and certain educational uses. Some countries have also enacted exceptions and limitations that expand access to copyrighted works to persons with visual disabilities, such as the provision of Braille copies.[4] These statutory provisions help states to achieve goals that IP law shares with human rights law.

Nonetheless, there are important divergences in the orientation of the two regimes. As compared to IP laws and treaties, human rights instruments emphasize societal goals over private economic interests. In

---

Application No. 73049/01, Eur. Ct. Hum. Rts. (Grand Chamber 2007). The right of property does not, however, appear in any UN human rights treaty. Further, even in Europe, as the UN Special Rapporteur in the Field of Cultural Rights has noted, the right of property merely obliges states to respect the IP rights they have recognized; it does not require them to create such rights or to adopt any particular approach to protecting IP. *Copyright Policy and the Right to Science and Culture, Report of the Special Rapporteur in the Field of Cultural Rights*, Farida Shaheed, A/HRC/28/57 ¶ 53 (Dec. 2014) [hereinafter SR Copyright Report].

4. WORLD INTELLECTUAL PROPERTY ORGANIZATION, STUDY ON COPYRIGHT LIMITATIONS AND EXCEPTIONS FOR THE VISUALLY IMPAIRED, SCCR/15/7 (2007) (prepared by Judith Sullivan) [hereinafter WIPO STUDY], http://www.wipo.int/edocs/mdocs/copyright/en/sccr_15/sccr_15_7.pdf.

addition, at the international level, the stronger enforcement mechanisms of IP treaties—such as in the TRIPS Agreement and in other recently negotiated bilateral, regional, and plurilateral IP treaties—have led states to emphasize IP protection without sufficiently considering its impact on human rights. For example, threats of economic sanctions or WTO complaints create incentives for states to enact copyright laws with fewer exceptions and limitations than may be needed to fully realize human rights.

Partly as a result of these pressures, many states have not taken full advantage of the flexibilities recognized in international IP law to ensure adequate access to copyrighted works. For example, prior to the adoption of the Marrakesh Treaty, only 57 countries had enacted an exception to copyright permitting persons with print disabilities to create accessible format copies.[5] The limited number of states adopting such an exception has been an important factor contributing to the book famine mentioned in the Introduction to this Guide.

1.1.4. Using Copyright Tools to Achieve Human Rights Ends

The Marrakesh Treaty uses the specific policy tool of exceptions and limitations to copyright to expand the global availability of accessible format copies of books and cultural materials. Such exceptions and limitations are found in all national laws. For example, most states permit certain uses of copyrighted material by libraries and educational institutions without the permission of the copyright owner. Some countries have broader and more flexible doctrines of fair use or fair dealing. Whatever approach a country follows, exceptions and limitations "constitute a vital part of the balance that copyright law must strike between the interests of rights-holders in exclusive control and the interests of others in cultural participation."[6]

International human rights instruments also recognize the societal benefits of exceptions and limitations. Most notably, the CRPD requires ratifying states to revise IP laws and adopt other policies to facilitate access

---

5. *Id.* at 9.
6. SR Copyright Report, *supra* note 3, ¶ 61.

to cultural materials. Article 30(1) of the CRPD requires states to "take all appropriate measures to ensure that persons with disabilities ... [e]njoy access to cultural materials in accessible formats," and Article 30(3) obligates states to "take all appropriate steps, in accordance with international law, to ensure that laws protecting intellectual property rights do not constitute an unreasonable or discriminatory barrier to access by persons with disabilities to cultural materials."[7]

The CRPD Committee has repeatedly called on states to ratify and implement the Marrakesh Treaty.[8] In a 2013 General Comment focused on the principle of accessibility, the Committee stressed the cross-border human rights impact of the MT.[9] The UN Special Rapporteur in the Field of Cultural Rights has also urged states to ratify the MT and to "ensure that their copyright laws contain adequate exceptions to facilitate the

---

7. Other international and regional instruments identify the importance of exceptions to copyright to achieving human rights goals. The European Union's InfoSoc Directive provides that "Member States should be given the option of providing for certain exceptions or limitations for cases such as ... for use by people with disabilities" and that "[i]t is in any case important for the Member States to adopt all necessary measures to facilitate access to works by persons suffering from a disability which constitutes an obstacle to the use of the works themselves, and to pay particular attention to accessible formats." Directive 2001/29/EC of the European Parliament and of the Council of 22 May 2001 on the harmonisation of certain aspects of copyright and related rights in the information society, ¶¶ 34, 43 [hereinafter InfoSoc Directive]. The Council of Europe has also called on Member States to "take appropriate steps ... to ensure that laws protecting intellectual property rights do not constitute an unreasonable or discriminatory barrier to access by people with disabilities to cultural materials, while respecting the provisions of international law." Council of Europe, Committee of Ministers Rec(2006)5, 3.2.3.vii (5 Apr. 2006).
8. The CRPD Committee has included this call for ratification in reviewing reports from Denmark, New Zealand, Korea, Belgium, Ecuador, and Mexico. In a General Comment on the right to education, the Committee has also called on states to ratify and implement the MT. *General Comment No. 4: Article 24 (Right to inclusive education)*, U.N. Doc. No. CRPD/C/GC/4 (2 Sept. 2016), ¶ 22.
9. The General Comment asserts that the Marrakesh Treaty "should ensure access to cultural material without unreasonable or discriminatory barriers for persons with disabilities, including people with disabilities living abroad or as a member of a minority in another country and who speak or use the same language or means of communication, especially those facing challenges accessing classic print materials." Committee on the Rights of Persons with Disabilities, *General Comment No. 2: Article 9 (Accessibility)*, U.N. Doc. No. CRPD/C/GC/2 (22 May 2014), ¶ 45 [hereinafter General Comment No. 2].

availability of works in formats accessible to persons with visual impairments and other disabilities, such as deafness."[10]

Ratification and implementation of the Marrakesh Treaty is thus a concrete way for states to realize the obligations, set forth in the CRPD and in other human rights instruments, to remove barriers to the accessibility of cultural materials. Legislation proposed by the European Union to implement the MT underscores this point and recognizes the permissibility of limiting intellectual property to achieve human rights ends:

> The proposed Directive [and Regulation] support[] the right of persons with disabilities to benefit from measures designed to ensure their independence, social and occupational integration and participation in the life of the community, as enshrined in Article 26 of the Charter of Fundamental Rights of the European Union ('the Charter'). The Directive [and Regulation] also reflect[] the Union's commitments under the UNCRPD. The UNCRPD guarantees people with disabilities the right of access to information and the right to participate in cultural, economic and social life on an equal basis with others. In view of this, it is justified to restrict the property rights of rightholders in light with the Union's obligations under the Charter.[11]

As Chapter 2 of the Guide explains in more detail, the MT requires Contracting Parties to adopt exceptions and limitations in their national laws to enable the creation and dissemination of accessible format copies of certain copyrighted works and to share these works across borders. As

---

10. SR Copyright Report, *supra* note 3, ¶ 116.
11. Proposal for a Regulation of the European Parliament and of the Council on the cross-border exchange between the Union and third countries of accessible format copies of certain works and other subject-matter protected by copyright and related rights for the benefit of persons who are blind, visually impaired or otherwise print disabled, COM(2016) 595 final, 2016/0279 (COD) (Sept. 14, 2016), p. 5; Proposal for a Directive of the European Parliament and of the Council on certain permitted uses of works and other subject-matter protected by copyright and related rights for the benefit of persons who are blind, visually impaired or otherwise print disabled and amending Directive 2001/29/EC on the harmonisation of certain aspects of copyright and related rights in the information society, COM(2016) 596 final, 2016/0278 (COD) (Sept. 14, 2016), p. 6.

previously noted, only 57 countries had adopted some version of these exceptions and limitations prior to the negotiation of the MT. A central objective of the Treaty, therefore, is to encourage all states to adopt a common set of exceptions and limitations to enhance the human rights of print-disabled persons.

1.2. INTERPRETIVE PRINCIPLES FOR THE MARRAKESH TREATY

This subsection identifies a set of principles for interpreting the MT as a treaty that promotes human rights objectives using the legal and policy tools of copyright. It also explains how these principles should guide the choices that government officials make in implementing the Treaty.

1.2.1. *Emphasize Object and Purpose*

The overarching goal of treaty interpretation is to give effect to the objective intent of the parties as manifested in the text of the treaty as a whole. The Vienna Convention on the Law of Treaties (VCLT) codifies customary international law rules governing the interpretation of treaties. Under Article 31(1) of the VCLT, a treaty is to be interpreted "in good faith in accordance with the ordinary meaning to be given to the terms of the treaty in their context and in the light of its object and purpose." Article 31 identifies three elements for interpreting a treaty—text, context, and object and purpose. None of these elements is to be given priority over any other. Treaty interpretation thus requires an interpreter to consider the specific clause at issue, other provisions such as the preamble, and what those terms and the context in which they appear reveal about the intention of the parties and the objectives of the agreement.

To identify the ordinary meaning of a particular treaty provision, an interpreter may consider common uses of terms, dictionary definitions, the grammar and syntax of the provision, as well as the use of the same or similar language elsewhere in the treaty. The ordinary meaning must also be understood in light of the context of the treaty as a whole. Under VCLT Article 31(2), the context of the treaty includes the text of the entire treaty, the preamble, any annexes, and "[a]ny agreement relating to the treaty which was made between all the parties in connection with the conclusion of the treaty." For example, the thirteen "Agreed Statements" in the footnotes of the Marrakesh Treaty are an integral part of the MT's context and thus relevant to understanding the ordinary meaning of its terms.[12]

Consistent with its focus on the parties' objective intent, the VCLT permits interpreters to consider drafting history—the documents associated with the negotiation of the treaty—only in specified circumstances. Article 32 allows recourse to the treaty's preparatory work and the circumstances of the treaty's conclusion, either "to confirm the meaning" that results from application of the primary principles of interpretation, or "to determine the meaning" when the interpretation in the ordinary course "(a) leaves the meaning ambiguous or obscure; or (b) leads to a result which is manifestly absurd or unreasonable." Thus, if it is not possible to identify a reasonable interpretation from the ordinary meaning of the terms in context and in light of the treaty's purpose, it would be appropriate to refer to the drafting history. The VCLT gives the drafting history a supplementary role in treaty interpretation because it can be unreliable evidence of the agreement's meaning. Most notably, the records of negotiations are often incomplete or may not reflect the political compromises that were made to adopt the agreement.

The VCLT also requires that text be interpreted in ways that promote the treaty's object and purpose.[13] The object and purpose include both the specific legal consequences contemplated in the agreement as well as

---

12. It is also possible to consider the CRPD as a "relevant rule[ ]" of international law applicable in the relations between the parties" to be taken into account, together with the context of the treaty, under VCLT Article 31(3)(c). It is unclear whether the CRPD would need to be ratified by some, most, or all of the parties to the MT, have passed into customary law, or be accepted by all parties to the MT, to be considered a "relevant rule." RICHARD K. GARDINER, TREATY INTERPRETATION 302–04, 310–17 (2d ed. 2015). As explained below, however, the CRPD is an important reference point for interpreting the MT regardless of whether it qualifies as a "relevant rule" under VCLT Article 31(3)(c).

13. The central role of object and purpose in interpreting treaties, particularly those designed to protect individuals, has been repeatedly affirmed by international tribunals. *See, e.g., Reservations to the Convention on the Prevention and Punishment of the Crime of Genocide*, 1951 I.C.J. 15, 23; *Proposed Amendments to the Naturalization Provisions of the Constitution of Costa Rica*, 1984 Inter-Am. Court H.R. (ser. A) No. 4, ¶ 23; *Hirsi Jamaa and Others v. Italy*, App. No. 27765/09, Eur. Ct. Hum. Rts., ¶ 171 (Grand Chamber 2012).

the overall goals of the parties.[14] An interpreter should look to the treaty as a whole to ascertain its object and purpose. However, consulting the preamble is often one of the best ways to identify a treaty's aims because these introductory clauses typically indicate why governments negotiated the agreement.

States are also required to implement the MT in ways that ensure that its provisions are effective. Effective interpretation is a general principle, or canon of construction, that guides the interpretation of all international agreements. Under this principle, it is reasonable for the interpreter to assume that the parties "intend the provisions of the treaty to have a certain effect, and not to be meaningless."[15] Thus, all other things being equal, an interpreter should choose an interpretation that renders a term effective in achieving the treaty's object and purpose over an interpretation that does not.

The MT's overarching object and purpose is to promote the human rights of individuals with print disabilities by expanding their access to copyrighted works consistently with existing rules of international IP law. Several features of the Treaty support this conclusion. First, as its title proclaims, the Treaty seeks *"to Facilitate Access* to Published Works for Persons Who Are Blind, Visually Impaired, or Otherwise Print Disabled" (emphasis added). Second, the Preamble explicitly references the UDHR and the CRPD and reiterates the parties' desire "to harmonize limitations and exceptions [to copyright] with a view to facilitating access to and use of works by persons with visual impairments or other print disabilities."[16] Third, the MT expressly identifies print-disabled individuals

---

14. EIRIK BJORGE, THE EVOLUTIONARY INTERPRETATION OF TREATIES 113 (2014).
15. OPPENHEIM'S INTERNATIONAL LAW, VOLUME 1 (PEACE) 1280 (Robert Jennings & Arthur Watts eds., 9th ed. 2008).
16. These references underscore that the MT helps states to achieve the accessibility goals of international human rights law, including the obligation in CRPD Article 30(3) to "ensure that laws protecting intellectual property rights do not constitute an unreasonable or discriminatory barrier to access by persons with disabilities to cultural materials." *See also* Draft Protocol to the African Charter on Human and Peoples' Rights on the Rights of Persons with Disabilities in Africa, adopted on February 25, 2016, Article 19.2(d), http://www.achpr.org/files/news/2016/04/d216/disability_protocol.pdf (requiring states to ensure that "persons with visual impairments or with other print disabilities have effective access to published works, including . . . by making changes as appropriate to the international copyright system").

as "beneficiary persons," underscoring the centrality of their human rights to achieving the Treaty's aims. Finally, unlike other IP treaties, the MT does not expand the rules of copyright protection; rather, it requires ratifying states to adopt mandatory exceptions to copyright and identifies those exceptions as presumptively compatible with existing international IP rules.

For all of these reasons, states and other actors should interpret and implement the Marrakesh Treaty to further its object and purpose of enhancing the availability of accessible format copies to print-disabled persons. Although the MT uses the doctrines and policies of copyright law to achieve this goal, the Treaty's fundamental aim is to enhance the human rights of these individuals. When deciding how to give effect to the MT, therefore, states should interpret the MT in ways that advance this object and purpose.[17] Chapter 2 of the Guide identifies specific policy proposals and recommendations consistent with this approach.

1.2.2. Adapt the Marrakesh Treaty to Changing Conditions

The Marrakesh Treaty should be interpreted and implemented in light of contemporary circumstances and in ways that respond to changes in law, policy, and technology. Decision-makers should give a treaty term an evolutionary meaning (rather than the meaning fixed at the time of the instrument's adoption) if it appears from the text, context, and object and purpose that the meaning should evolve over time. For example, a generic term may indicate that the drafters intended the meaning to evolve over time to take account of present-day conditions and challenges. A term may also be read in light of current conditions to account for new technological developments or other circumstances the drafters did not or could not have considered. These evolutionary approaches help to ensure that a treaty remains effective in realizing its object and purpose.

---

17. For treaties that are designed to protect individuals, interpretations that are more protective are to be favored over those that are less protective. Rudolf Bernhardt, *Evolutive Treaty Interpretation, Especially of the European Convention on Human Rights*, 42 GERMAN Y.B. INT'L L. 11, 14 (1999).

With regard to the MT, states will need to interpret and implement the rights of print-disabled individuals in light of new technologies and evolving meanings of disability. The objective intent of the Treaty's drafters was to ensure that individuals with print disabilities can make and share accessible format copies even as the methods of copying and distribution change over time. This is implied by the text of the Treaty, which defines "accessible format copy" by reference to whether a copy is accessible rather than by reference to any particular technology. As a result, states should not restrict exceptions and limitations to existing formats or particular technologies. Rather, implementing legislation should be open-ended to explicitly encompass technologies that may be developed in the future. An open-ended definition also ensures the broadest possible access to copyrighted works. Thus, although states may provide examples of accessible format copies (e.g., large print, digital text, e-books, among others) in implementing legislation, they should expressly indicate that these examples are illustrative rather than exhaustive.

1.2.3. Promote Consistency with the CRPD

One of the MT's objectives, as set forth in the Preamble, is to realize the "principles of non-discrimination, equal opportunity, accessibility and full and effective participation and inclusion in society" protected in the CRPD and the UDHR. These cross references reveal that the MT embodies many of the same core principles and values embraced by the CRPD. Moreover, given that more than 85 percent of UN member states have ratified the CRPD, most MT ratifying countries will have already joined the CRPD. As a result, the interpretations of the CRPD Committee can help guide states in making choices that fulfill the MT's object and purpose.[18] This subsection discusses the origin of the CRPD and the core principles developed by the CRPD Committee that animate the convention.[19]

---

18. States may have obligations under other human rights treaties to ensure the accessibility of cultural materials for individuals with print disabilities. *See, e.g.,* Committee on Economic, Social and Cultural Rights, *General Comment No. 5 (Persons with disabilities),* U.N. Doc E/1995/22 (1994), ¶ 5.
19. Trade tribunals have also stressed the importance of integrating different international regimes. *E.g., United States—Import Prohibition of Certain Shrimp and Shrimp Products,* WT/DS58/AB/R (1998), ¶ 129 (emphasizing that exceptions to free trade rules "must

1.2.3.1. BACKGROUND TO THE CRPD

The CRPD is a legally binding human rights agreement aimed at promoting and protecting the rights of individuals with disabilities. It entered into force on May 3, 2008 and is accompanied by an Optional Protocol that authorizes individuals and groups to file communications alleging violations of the CRPD by states that have ratified the Optional Protocol. As of October 2016, 168 countries have ratified the CRPD and 92 countries have ratified the Optional Protocol. The CRPD Committee, a treaty body created by the convention, reviews these communications and reports from all States Parties regarding implementation of the convention. The Committee reports to the UN General Assembly about its work.

The impetus for adopting the CRPD was the recognition that the rights of individuals with physical and mental disabilities, although already implicit in other international human rights instruments, were not adequately realized or protected. The CRPD builds on these preexisting instruments by articulating rights with greater precision and by providing more specific descriptions of state duties. In particular, the CRPD emphasizes that disabled persons possess human rights that states are obligated to realize, requires the provision of remedies to individuals whose rights have been violated, and mandates the involvement of disabled persons in the creation and implementation of laws, policies, and technologies that affect their rights.

1.2.3.2. CENTRAL PRINCIPLES OF THE CRPD

Accessibility and non-discrimination are central interpretive principles of the CRPD and, by extension, of the MT, which seeks to realize, in part, the rights outlined in the CRPD.

Accessibility. A central purpose of the CRPD is to enable the participation of individuals with disabilities in all aspects of society. Article 1 provides that the convention's purpose is "to promote, protect and ensure the

---

be read by a treaty interpreter in the light of contemporary concerns of the community of nations"); *European Communities and Certain Member States—Measures Affecting Trade in Large Civil Aircraft*, WT/DS316/AB/R (2011), ¶ 845 (stressing the "principle of systemic integration which . . . seeks to ensure that international obligations are interpreted by reference to their normative environment in a manner that gives coherence and meaningfulness to the process of legal interpretation") (internal citations and quotations omitted).

full and equal enjoyment of all human rights and fundamental freedoms by all persons with disabilities, and to promote respect for their inherent dignity." Paragraphs "e" and "y" of the Preamble identify as two of the convention's goals contributing to eliminating the social disadvantage experienced by persons with disabilities and promoting their full participation in all spheres of life in both developed and developing countries.

Accessibility of the physical, social, economic, and cultural environment is a critical precondition for disabled individuals to participate fully in society and to enjoy their rights. The emphasis on accessibility reflects the social model of disability that underlies the CRPD. This model recognizes that disability does not result from an individual's physical or mental condition but is rather the product of environmental barriers that prevent an individual with an impairment from fully participating in society on a basis of equality with others. (CRPD, Preamble.) A rights-based approach to disability requires the state to remove barriers to the enjoyment of rights and to create the conditions needed for all individuals to participate meaningfully in society. The importance of accessibility has been reaffirmed by the CRPD Committee, which has devoted a General Comment to this principle. According to the Committee, accessibility is a precondition for the realization and enjoyment of rights protected under the CRPD.[20] For example, access to information is a precondition for the realization of the rights to freedom of expression, to education, and to participation in culture.[21]

Several articles of the CRPD expressly require states to take steps to ensure access to printed works. These include provisions that protect access to information and communications (Article 9), freedom of expression (Article 21), the right to education (Article 24), and the right to participate in cultural life (Article 30).[22] More specifically, Article 30

---

20. General Comment No. 2, *supra* note 9, ¶ 36.
21. *Id.* ¶¶ 38, 39, 44.
22. These rights are also protected by other treaties, including the ICCPR and ICESCR. The right to take part in cultural life, for example, is guaranteed by Article 15.1(a) of the ICESCR. The CRPD provides a more detailed description of what that right means for individuals with disabilities and what duties states have in realizing the right—which in this case includes the obligation to ensure that IP laws do not prevent individuals with disabilities from participating in culture. CRPD, art. 30(3). Thus, although the CRPD makes this more explicit, a state that had ratified the ICESCR but not the CRPD would still be

requires states to modify copyright and other IP laws to facilitate access to cultural materials—an obligation the CRPD Committee has indicated can be satisfied in part by joining the Marrakesh Treaty.[23]

Non-Discrimination. Non-discrimination is a core principle of international human rights law and the cornerstone of every human rights treaty. The focus on equality in the CRPD is emphasized in Article 1, which notes that the convention's purpose is to "promote, protect and ensure the full and equal enjoyment of all human rights and fundamental freedoms by all persons with disabilities." Article 4 obligates states to take all appropriate measures to change laws and policies in order to eliminate discrimination against people with disabilities.

Discrimination exists when a state fails to ensure accessibility or to remove barriers that prevent individuals from enjoying their rights on an equal basis with others. As the CRPD Committee has explained, the state's duty to ensure access to information and communication must be understood in light of the obligation to avoid discrimination. "Denial of access to . . . information and communication . . . constitutes an act of disability-based discrimination that is prohibited by article 5 of the Convention."[24]

In its General Comment No. 2, the CRPD Committee makes explicit the close relationship between accessibility and non-discrimination. According to the Committee, Article 9's commitment to ensuring that individuals with disabilities have equal access to goods and services "stems from the prohibition against discrimination; denial of access should be considered to constitute a discriminatory act, regardless of whether the perpetrator is a public or private entity."[25] Thus, in discussing state

---

required to eliminate barriers that prevent individuals with print disabilities from accessing cultural materials, including barriers created by IP law.

23. General Comment No. 2, *supra* note 9, ¶ 45.
24. *Id.* ¶ 34.
25. *Id.* ¶ 13. In the General Comment, the Committee explicitly links the obligations in Article 9 regarding accessibility with the prohibition on non-discrimination in Article 5. *Id.* ¶ 34 (denial of access, including to information and communication, "constitutes an act of disability-based discrimination that is prohibited by article 5 of the Convention"); *cf. Szilvia Nyusti and Péter Takács v. Hungary (Views)*, Communication No. 1/2010, U.N. Doc. No. CRPD/C/9/D/1/2010 (21 June 2013), ¶ 9.4 (noting the conceptual connection between accessibility and non-discrimination in finding a violation of Article 9 based on the state's failure to ensure the accessibility of bank ATMs).

obligations, the Committee notes explicitly that "[d]enial of access should be clearly defined as a prohibited act of discrimination."[26] As applied to the Marrakesh Treaty, the principles of accessibility and non-discrimination direct ratifying countries to facilitate the availability of covered copyrighted works in a wide array of accessible formats, and to ensure that print-disabled individuals can access, enjoy, and share copyrighted works on substantially the same terms as fully sighted persons.

1.2.3.3. CONSULTATIONS WITH STAKEHOLDERS

An important provision in the CRPD is the obligation to consult with affected individuals and groups, including with regard to implementing treaty obligations in domestic law and policy. This consultation requirement appears in Article 4(3) of the convention, which provides:

> In the development and implementation of legislation and policies to implement the present Convention, and in other decision-making processes concerning issues relating to persons with disabilities, States Parties shall closely consult with and actively involve persons with disabilities, including children with disabilities, through their representative organizations.

The obligation to consult does not end with the adoption of implementing legislation. CRPD Article 33(3) provides that civil society groups, disability rights organizations, and persons with disabilities "shall be involved and participate fully in the monitoring process" of the convention. Consultations provide the government with crucial input in drafting appropriate legislation and regulations, and help it to identify and surmount barriers to realizing the CRPD's objectives.

To ensure consistency with the CRPD and other human rights treaties, states that ratify the Marrakesh Treaty should consult with print-disabled individuals, and with organizations that advocate for and provide services to those individuals, at all stages of the implementation process. These stages include preparing and reviewing implementing legislation,

---

26. General Comment No. 2, *supra* note 9, ¶ 29.

identifying appropriate monitoring institutions, evaluating whether the Treaty's access and sharing provisions are actually being utilized, and preparing reports to international human rights bodies. To facilitate broad participation in these activities, governments should make all relevant documents and proceedings available in accessible formats.

States should also consult with print-disabled individuals both when designing legislation to incorporate the MT in domestic laws and policies, and when monitoring how those laws and policies operate in practice. For example, states with greater administrative capacity might launch a consultation process in connection with the drafting of implementing legislation, inviting disability rights organizations to submit proposals for new laws and regulations, attend public hearings on draft legislation, and testify before or make written submissions to parliamentary committees considering such legislation. States with more limited capacity might form a steering group composed of print-disabled individuals and their representative organizations to provide input to the government as it implements the MT.

The obligation to consult regarding MT monitoring processes could include, for example, involving authorized entities and disability rights organizations in the design of empirical studies to determine whether MT-required exceptions and limitations in copyright laws are in fact expanding the availability and cross-border exchange of accessible format copies. Such groups are also crucial partners for raising awareness about the rights provided by the MT—awareness that encourages policy-relevant feedback regarding the effective implementation of the Treaty.

Chapter 2

The Legal and Policy Choices in the Marrakesh Treaty

As discussed in Chapter 1, a central objective of the Marrakesh Treaty is to facilitate the creation, sharing, and distribution of accessible format copies for the benefit of print-disabled individuals. To accomplish this goal, the MT requires ratifying states to amend their national laws to include a variety of exceptions and limitations to the exclusive rights of copyright holders. Chapter 2 of this Guide provides an article-by-article overview of the MT's core provisions and offers guidance for interpreting and implementing those provisions in ways that are consistent with the Treaty's objectives. Each topic begins with a brief overview followed by the text of the relevant provision. We then provide a detailed analysis of the text and recommendations for how states should incorporate the relevant obligations into their respective national laws.

2.1. COPYRIGHTED WORKS COVERED BY THE MARRAKESH TREATY

The Marrakesh Treaty applies to a broad category of works protected by copyright. In particular, Article 2(a) provides that exceptions and limitations for the benefit of print-disabled individuals apply to particular "literary and artistic works"—a term of art defined in international copyright law. However, the MT goes beyond that definition by emphasizing that the Treaty applies to such works regardless of the media in which they appear.

> TEXT OF THE MARRAKESH TREATY
>
> Article 2(a): "works" means literary and artistic works within the meaning of Article 2(1) of the Berne Convention for the Protection of Literary and Artistic Works, in the form of text, notation and/or related illustrations, whether published or otherwise made publicly available in any media.

The phrase "literary and artistic works" defined in Article 2(1) of the Berne Convention is extremely broad. It includes "every production in the literary, scientific and artistic domain," with the exception of audiovisual works. Specific copyrighted works in Article 2(1) that are therefore protected under the Marrakesh Treaty include: "books, pamphlets and other writings; lectures, addresses, sermons and other works of the same nature; dramatic or dramatico-musical works," as well as "illustrations, maps, plans, sketches."

Article 2(1) of the Berne Convention underscores that a literary or artistic work is eligible for copyright protection "whatever may be the mode or form of its expression." Article 2(a) of the MT incorporates this phrase by reference and expands its scope. Specifically, Article 2(a) clarifies that literary and artistic works are covered by the MT regardless of whether they are "published or otherwise made publicly available in any media." The Agreed Statement to Article 2(a) also makes clear that literary and artistic works "includes such works in audio form, such as audiobooks."

The provisions described above yield two primary insights. First, the MT applies to both published and unpublished works. Thus, a print-disabled individual can make and share accessible format copies of works that are considered unpublished under national law. Second, it means that MT rights are technology neutral. Print-disabled individuals can make and share copyrighted works regardless of the media or technological format in which those works appear. Thus, for example, a state that ratifies the MT must provide exceptions and limitations enabling beneficiary persons to make and share not only audiobooks but also "born digital" works originating in a digital form, such as e-books, wikis, electronic records, and webcomics.[27]

2.2. ACCESSIBLE FORMAT COPIES

A central feature of the MT is the authorization for beneficiary persons and authorized entities (defined in the next subsection of the Guide) to create accessible format copies. Article 2(b) of the MT defines "accessible format copy" in flexible and format-neutral terms to ensure that print-disabled individuals may use whatever format will provide them with access that is as feasible and comfortable as that enjoyed by non-print-disabled individuals.

TEXT OF THE MARRAKESH TREATY

Article 2(b): "accessible format copy" means a copy of a work in an alternative manner or form which gives a beneficiary person access to the work, including to permit the person to have access as feasibly and comfortably as a person without visual impairment or other print disability. The accessible format copy is used exclusively by beneficiary persons and it must respect the integrity of the original work, taking due consideration of the changes needed to make the work accessible in the alternative format and of the accessibility needs of the beneficiary persons.

---

27. *See* Ricky Erway, *Defining "Born Digital,"* Online Computer Library Center (Nov. 2010), http://www.oclc.org/content/dam/research/activities/hiddencollections/borndigital.pdf.

Article 2(b) makes clear that beneficiary persons and authorized entities may make a copy of a covered copyrighted work in any manner or form needed to ensure access. In particular, the MT does not limit the making of copies of such works to special formats, such as Braille, that are traditionally used only by print-disabled individuals. To the contrary, "accessible format copy" is defined as a copy made in a "manner or form which gives a beneficiary person access to the work." Depending on the individual and his or her disability, this may include formats that can also be used by non-print-disabled individuals—such as an e-book or audiobook.[28] Limiting the MT to copies that can *only* be used by print-disabled individuals—as one commentator appears to suggest[29]—would unreasonably exclude from the MT's benefits all disabled persons who do not or cannot use such special formats.

Several additional considerations underscore the importance of the flexible, format-neutral approach adopted by Article 2(b). First, it is impossible to predict in advance the specific needs of all individuals with print disabilities. The particular format or formats that enable such individuals to access a work "as feasibly and comfortably" as a non-print-disabled individual—whether e-book, audiobook, DAISY, or EPUB3—will depend on the particular type of disability and its interaction with other physical or mental conditions, among other factors. Second, a flexible, format-neutral approach ensures that the MT will evolve to take into account the emergence of new technologies. States should therefore expressly include a flexible, format-neutral definition in national implementing legislation, both to encompass future technological evolution and to promote the accessibility of covered works.

2.3. AUTHORIZED ENTITIES

2.3.1. Introduction and Overview

To ensure that individuals with print disabilities enjoy broad access to literary and artistic works, the MT empowers a variety of actors to create

---

28. The Agreed Statement concerning Article 2(a) defines "works" as including "audio form, such as audiobooks."
29. *See* Mihály J. Ficsor, *Commentary to the Marrakesh Treaty on Accessible Format Copies for the Visually Impaired* at 15, ¶ 6 (2013).

and share accessible format copies. These actors include not only "beneficiary persons" themselves (a phrase analyzed in detail below), but also a "primary caretaker or caregiver" of such a person, as well as anyone "acting on ... behalf" of a beneficiary person. (Article 4(2)(b).) This expansive list reflects the reality that many print-disabled individuals require assistance to engage in daily life activities, including accessing and reading books and consuming cultural materials.

In recognition of these challenges, the MT also designates an additional category of actors—known as "authorized entities"—to assist print-disabled persons. Authorized entities are entitled to make accessible format copies, obtain such copies from other beneficiaries and authorized entities, and distribute or make available those copies to beneficiary persons and to authorized entities in other countries. Authorized entities are thus crucial to achieving the MT's overarching objective of overcoming the considerable barriers that print-disabled individuals currently face in making and sharing accessible format copies.

This section of the Guide analyzes the phrase "authorized entity" as defined in Article 2(c) of the MT. As explained below, such entities may be government or public institutions or non-profit organizations or groups that provide a range of services to individuals with print disabilities. Some authorized entities primarily serve print-disabled communities. However, the MT recognizes a much larger group of public and non-profit groups and bodies—including schools, libraries, healthcare organizations, and civil society groups—whose activities are intended to benefit society as a whole, including individuals with print disabilities.

In addition, Article 2(c) defines an authorized entity as an entity that creates and follows its own practices to, among other things, ensure that the persons it serves are beneficiary persons. An authorized entity is required to limit its distribution of accessible format copies to beneficiary persons or other authorized entities. The MT leaves it to authorized entities themselves to develop and monitor these practices. For this reason, and because of the diversity of organizations and groups that can qualify as authorized entities, a wide variety of practices will be consistent with Article 2(c).

> **TEXT OF THE MARRAKESH TREATY**
>
> <u>Article 2(c)</u>: "authorized entity" means an entity that is authorized or recognized by the government to provide education, instructional training, adaptive reading or information access to beneficiary persons on a non-profit basis. It also includes a government institution or non-profit organization that provides the same services to beneficiary persons as one of its primary activities or institutional obligations.
>
> An authorized entity establishes and follows its own practices:
> (i) to establish that the persons it serves are beneficiary persons;
> (ii) to limit to beneficiary persons and/or authorized entities its distribution and making available of accessible format copies;
> (iii) to discourage the reproduction, distribution and making available of unauthorized copies; and
> (iv) to maintain due care in, and records of, its handling of copies of works, while respecting the privacy of beneficiary persons in accordance with Article 8 [on respect for privacy].

2.3.2. *Types of Authorized Entities*

The MT defines authorized entities principally by reference to the services that they provide to individuals with print disabilities. Article 2(c) lists four distinct services—(1) education, (2) instructional training, (3) adaptive reading, or (4) information access. Each service is separated by the word "or," which means that an organization or group that engages in only one of these activities still qualifies as an authorized entity (although it may carry out multiple activities). The service or services the organization or group offers must be provided on a non-profit basis. For-profit private entities—such as for-profit universities and schools, medical facilities, and Internet service providers—do not qualify as authorized entities even if they provide one or more of the listed services to persons with print disabilities. (As noted below, however, a for-profit organization may be an authorized entity if it is authorized or recognized by the government.)

The Treaty does not define the terms "non-profit" or "for-profit"; accordingly, this determination will be made under each state's applicable domestic laws. However, non-profit status does not preclude an authorized entity from charging a fee for making or sharing accessible format copies, for example, to cover its expenses. Restrictions, if any, on the fees that authorized entities can charge for performing these services will also be determined by each state's domestic laws regulating the non-profit sector.

Although for-profit organizations generally do not qualify as authorized entities under the MT, this does not mean that these entities are prohibited from making accessible format copies and sharing them with print-disabled persons, with or without charging a fee. Such services, however, need to be justified under copyright exceptions other than those required by the MT, or under other national laws, such as legislation protecting the rights of disabled persons.

Authorized entities can be—but are not required to be—recognized by the government. As explained below, an authorized entity can be any group or organization that provides services to beneficiaries. This is made explicit in the first two sentences of Article 2(c), which describe two distinct types of authorized entities—organizations recognized by a government, and organizations without such recognition. A recognition process may help to provide assurances to organizations or groups that they are entitled to make and share accessible copies. However, any such process must avoid burdening authorized entities or chilling unrecognized organizations from exercising rights under the MT.

2.3.2.1. ENTITIES PROVIDING SERVICES TO BENEFICIARIES

Any non-profit organization or group is entitled to make and share accessible format copies if it provides one of the listed services to beneficiary persons. As stated earlier, an organization or group does not need to be recognized by or otherwise obtain permission from the government in order to make and share accessible format copies as part of the services it provides to print-disabled individuals. This is apparent from the second sentence of Article 2(c), which refers to any "non-profit organization that provides [covered] services to beneficiary persons." The Agreed Statement to Article 9 further underscores this conclusion, rejecting "mandatory registration" as "a precondition for authorized entities to engage in activities recognized under this Treaty."[30]

Consistent with this view, any organization that provides one or more services listed in Article 2(c) can act as an authorized entity and carry out all of the activities permitted by the MT without government approval or the permission of copyright owners. Authorized entities encompass organizations whose mission is to assist print-disabled individuals with services such as education, instructional training, and accessible format printed works and cultural materials. Such groups include, for example, the World Blind Union, similar global advocacy organizations and their regional and national affiliates, schools, libraries, and printing houses that primarily serve persons with print disabilities.

The MT does not, however, limit authorized entities to groups that primarily serve persons with print disabilities. To the contrary, providing services to print-disabled persons need only be "*one of* [the group's] primary activities or institutional obligations." (Article 2(c) (emphasis added).) This phrase should be interpreted broadly to include educational institutions, libraries, healthcare organizations, civil society groups, and other governmental or non-profit organizations that are open to the general public or that serve a broader membership or client base—if one of their primary activities is providing a service listed in Article 2(c). For example, interpreting language in U.S. law that is narrower than the MT, the federal district court in *Authors Guild, Inc. v. HathiTrust* nonetheless found that libraries of general educational institutions have a primary mission to distribute materials to print-disabled individuals and thus qualify as authorized entities under the Chafee Amendment to the 1976 Copyright Act—the exception benefitting print-disabled individuals in the United States.[31]

---

30. The Agreed Statement concerning Article 9 provides: "It is understood that Article 9 does not imply mandatory registration for authorized entities nor does it constitute a precondition for authorized entities to engage in activities recognized under this Treaty; but it provides for a possibility for sharing information to facilitate the cross-border exchange of accessible format copies."
31. *Authors Guild, Inc. v. HathiTrust*, 902 F. Supp. 2d 445, 465 (S.D.N.Y. 2012), *aff'd in part and vacated in part on other grounds*, 755 F.3d 87 (2d Cir. 2014).

Including organizations that serve the general public as "authorized entities" furthers the MT's human rights objectives in multiple ways. The more generous funding that many such organizations receive allows them to provide more extensive or lower-cost services to print-disabled individuals. The inclusion also enables beneficiary persons to be educated and trained in the same institutions as individuals without print disabilities, facilitating social integration. For these reasons, states should encourage general purpose organizations to serve as authorized entities and should clearly reflect that policy in national implementing legislation.

2.3.2.2. GOVERNMENT RECOGNIZED ENTITIES

Authorized entities can also be organizations that are explicitly recognized or approved by the government to make and share accessible format copies. Entities in this category could be public institutions, such as a bureau within a government ministry or a public library. They may also be private, non-profit institutions, such as disability rights groups or advocacy organizations. Finally, this category includes for-profit entities, such as a for-profit prison that is recognized by the government as providing services to print-disabled individuals.

Governments may adopt a process for these bodies to apply for recognition or establish criteria that, if satisfied, presumptively confer recognition upon such entities. These processes or criteria may be included in legislation or administrative regulations, or applied on a case-by-case basis. Whichever approach is adopted, the state should provide assurances that recognized entities are entitled to make and share accessible format copies without the permission of copyright holders, thereby deterring threats of copyright infringement lawsuits.

Governments that adopt a recognition or certification process must, however, ensure that any such process does not become a barrier for organizations that provide services to print-disabled individuals, including authorized entities not recognized by the government. For example, any such process must be easy to follow and avoid placing a financial burden on applicants. In addition, the government must clearly communicate to applicants, civil society groups, and the public that recognition is not necessary for an organization serving beneficiaries, as well as beneficiaries themselves, to make and share accessible format copies.

It is also important to distinguish government recognition from how an authorized entity is funded. As the Agreed Statement to Article 2(c) explains, recognized entities include but are not limited to "entities receiving financial support from the government."[32] So long as the organization or group is non-profit, the fact that it receives all, some, or none of its funding from the state does not affect its status as an authorized entity.

2.3.3. The Practices of Authorized Entities

The second half of Article 2(c) describes four practices that define authorized entities and that relate to the activities they perform under the MT, that is, making, accessing, and cross-border sharing or distribution of accessible format copies. Three of the four practices seek to ensure that these activities are carried out on behalf of beneficiary persons and other authorized entities, and that non-qualifying individuals, groups, and organizations do not benefit from these activities. The fourth practice directs authorized entities to exercise due care in processing and handling copies of works, to maintain records regarding such works, and to respect the privacy rights of beneficiary persons.

These four practices are cumulative; an authorized entity is defined as engaging in all of them. However, the Treaty does not prescribe the content of these practices. Instead, Article 2(c) permits each entity to "establish[] and follow[] its own practices." This language makes clear that the entity itself is responsible for creating and implementing these required practices in good faith. Nothing in the MT empowers governments to monitor or inspect the activities or records of authorized entities to verify that they are following the four practices (although other domestic laws or regulations may confer such authority).[33]

---

32. The Agreed Statement concerning Article 2(c) provides: "For the purposes of this Treaty, it is understood that 'entities recognized by the government' may include entities receiving financial support from the government to provide education, instructional training, adaptive reading or information access to beneficiary persons on a non-profit basis."
33. THE MARRAKESH TREATY: AN EIFL GUIDE FOR LIBRARIES 5 (Dec. 2014) ("[A]ny library or institution that meets the broad criteria set out in Article 2(c) qualifies as an authorized entity.... [T]he treaty does not contemplate rules being established for it by the government, nor an approval process or mechanism.").

This interpretation of Article 2(c) reflects the diverse array of authorized entities included in the MT and the practical impossibility of imposing a one-size-fits-all standard. It also means that governments should not impose mandatory accreditation or certification standards with regard to these practices. Such requirements could create undue practical or financial burdens, especially for entities in developing nations. It should thus be sufficient, at least in ordinary cases, for a resource-strapped entity in a developing country to adopt and follow its own practices.

2.4. BENEFICIARY PERSONS

2.4.1. Introduction and Overview

A core objective of the Marrakesh Treaty is to assist print-disabled individuals who are unable to access books and other cultural materials in traditional formats. The MT refers to these individuals as "beneficiary persons," a term that underscores the importance that the negotiators attached to enabling these individuals to create and share accessible format copies. This Guide uses the terms "print-disabled individuals" and "individuals with print disabilities" interchangeably to refer to the beneficiary persons protected by the Treaty. Consistent with the MT's overarching human rights objectives, the Guide also refers to these individuals as "rights holders"—persons who are legally entitled to create and share accessible format copies and to receive state assistance in doing so.

This section of the Guide analyzes the phrase "beneficiary persons" in Article 3 of the MT and suggests how states should implement that provision in national law. As explained below, Article 3 encompasses three different categories of print-disabled persons. These categories are defined by reference to the functional and social barriers that prevent disabled individuals from accessing traditional printed works. The medical, physical, or other causes of these impairments—such as traumatic brain injury, dyslexia, or dementia—are not relevant to the definition of beneficiary persons.

If existing national law exceptions and limitations to copyright do not currently apply to all three categories of print-disabled individuals, a state that ratifies the MT must expand those provisions to comply with the Treaty. The simplest way to do this would be to track the language in Article 3. However, states may also choose to apply the MT to persons with disabilities in general, both in recognition of the fact that beneficiary persons often have other disabilities and to give effect to the CRPD and to other international law obligations.

TEXT OF THE MARRAKESH TREATY

Article 3
Beneficiary Persons

A beneficiary person is a person who:
(a) is blind;
(b) has a visual impairment or a perceptual or reading disability which cannot be improved to give visual function substantially equivalent to that of a person who has no such impairment or disability and so is unable to read printed works to substantially the same degree as a person without an impairment or disability; or
(c) is otherwise unable, through physical disability, to hold or manipulate a book or to focus or move the eyes to the extent that would be normally acceptable for reading;
regardless of any other disabilities.

2.4.2. *Categories of Beneficiary Persons*

Article 3 identifies three categories of beneficiary persons. These categories, which are listed in paragraphs (a), (b), and (c), are separated by the word "or." An individual who falls in only one of the three paragraphs qualifies as a beneficiary person (although some print-disabled persons may be covered by more than one category). In addition, the "regardless of any other disabilities" clause that ends Article 3 makes clear that print-disabled individuals who also experience other types of disabilities—such as mental, intellectual, or auditory impairments—qualify as beneficiary persons under the MT. Finally, the definition is not limited to permanent disabilities. Individuals who experience temporary blindness or visual impairment, perceptual or reading disability, or a physical disability that interferes with reading, are entitled to benefit from the MT for as long as that condition persists.

2.4.2.1. BLINDNESS

States may rely on preexisting definitions of blindness in their respective national laws to extend the MT to individuals referenced in paragraph (a). Many countries have adopted definitions of blindness that include persons who experience less than a total loss of visual acuity (the ability to discern letters and numbers at a given distance) or visual field (the area in which objects can be seen in peripheral vision). India, for example, has adopted both a simple definition (the inability to "count fingers from a distance of 6 meters or 20 feet") and a technical definition ("[v]ision of 6/60 or less with the best possible spectacle correction").[34] Canada follows a different approach, defining blindness as a best-corrected visual acuity of 20/200 or worse in the better eye, or a visual field of less than 20 degrees.[35]

These and other flexible definitions of blindness recognize that an individual can be functionally without sight even if he or she retains limited visual ability. The definitions also take account of the fact that many print-disabled adults acquire visual disabilities by degrees as they age. Inasmuch as nothing in the MT limits or qualifies the word "blind" in paragraph (a) of Article 3, these preexisting functional definitions of legal blindness should be understood as fully consistent with the Treaty. In addition, states should consider adjusting their national law definitions to reflect the flexible approach to "blindness" that the MT adopts.

2.4.2.2. VISUAL IMPAIRMENT OR PERCEPTUAL DISABILITY

The second category of beneficiary persons, defined in Article 3(b), includes individuals who have a visual impairment or a disability that relates either to perception or to reading. There are three important

---

34. Government of India, National Program for Control of Blindness, http://npcb.nic.in/index1.asp?linkid=55.
35. CNIB, Glossary of AMD Terms, http://www.cnib.ca/en/your-eyes/eye-conditions/amd/resources/glossary/Pages/default.aspx.

aspects of subsection (b). First, this part of the definition extends the MT to individuals whose visual impairments do not rise to the level of blindness but nevertheless leave them "unable to read printed works to substantially the same degree" as those without such an impairment or disability.

Second, subsection (b) extends the definition of beneficiaries to individuals with perceptual or reading disabilities. An individual who does not have a visual impairment but who experiences a reading disability, such as dyslexia, that prevents him or her from reading printed works to substantially the same degree as someone without that disability, is also a beneficiary person.

Third, the impairment or disability must not be readily capable of being improved such that the individual acquires visual function that substantially corresponds to the visual function of persons who do not have such an impairment or disability. For example, the MT would not apply to a person whose visual impairment can be corrected with eyeglasses, provided that such correction is physically and financially accessible to that individual.

It is important to understand the type of improvements that would lead print-disabled and non-print-disabled persons to have a "substantially equivalent" ability to read covered works. The MT's negotiators attached considerable importance to this issue, as reflected in the Agreed Statement clarifying the phrase "cannot be improved." The Agreed Statement provides that an individual remains covered by paragraph (b) even if theoretical or potential "medical diagnostic procedures and treatments" exist that would alleviate his or her impairment or disability.[36] This means, for example, that consistent with the human rights principle of autonomy, an individual does not cease to be a MT beneficiary simply because there is a possibility that his or her visual impairment could be improved by existing or future treatments or technologies.

Interpreted from a human rights perspective, paragraph (b)'s "cannot be improved" clause should not place an unreasonable burden on print-disabled individuals with limited financial means, including those

---

36. The Agreed Statement to Article 3(b) provides: "Nothing in this language implies that 'cannot be improved' requires the use of all possible medical diagnostic procedures and treatments."

in developing countries. In deciding whether an improvement is in fact "available," a State Party to the MT may thus take into account not only the state's level of economic development and its public health system, but also the affordability of the improvement to individuals with a visual impairment or a perceptual or reading disability.

The medical condition known as cataracts—in which the lens of the eye becomes progressively opaque—illustrates how Article 3(b) takes account of different levels of resources available to individuals in countries around the world. Early-stage cataracts can be treated with corrective eyeglasses. As the condition progresses, however, restoring vision usually requires surgery. In countries where such surgeries are not widely available or are financially inaccessible, a state could reasonably conclude that individuals with cataracts are covered by paragraph (b) because their impairment cannot realistically be improved. Even where such treatments are available and financially accessible, however, each ratifying state has the discretion to determine what constitutes an impairment that "cannot be improved," taking into account the needs of individual beneficiaries and relevant local contexts.[37]

2.4.2.3. PHYSICAL READING DISABILITY

The third category of beneficiary persons encompasses individuals whose physical disabilities prevent them from reading a traditional printed book or other publication. The physical disabilities referred to in this paragraph include the inability to hold or manipulate a book or to focus or move the eyes in a usual manner. Examples include quadriplegia, cerebral palsy, tremor, brain or spinal injury, or motor-neuron and neurodegenerative diseases such as amyotrophic lateral sclerosis (ALS). Individuals with these physical conditions experience challenges in accessing traditional reading materials similar to persons who are blind or have visual impairments.

---

37. *Cf. S.H. and Others v. Austria*, Application No. 57813/00 ¶ 97, Eur. Ct. Hum. Rts. (Grand Chamber 2011) (concluding that governments have a wide "margin of appreciation" (i.e., broad discretion) to regulate in vitro fertilization treatments given divergent national responses to "medical and scientific developments" and different ways to "achieve a balance between the competing public and private interests").

2.4.3. Defining Beneficiary Persons in Implementing Legislation

The categories of print-disabled individuals described in Article 3 provide a minimum standard for beneficiary persons protected by the MT. All ratifying states must meet this standard when implementing the Treaty. We describe below three issues that may arise when countries implement Article 3 and suggest how those issues should be resolved.

First, for states that have not previously adopted exceptions to copyright that benefit print-disabled individuals, the simplest way to implement Article 3 would be to track the language of its three paragraphs as written. Legislation that does not track that language risks narrowing the definition of beneficiary persons and thus not complying fully with its Marrakesh Treaty obligations. For example, Singapore adopted the Copyright (Amendment) Act 2014 prior to ratifying the MT in 2015. The Act defines a "person with a reading disability" as "(a) a blind person; (b) a person whose sight is severely impaired; (c) a person unable to hold or manipulate books or to focus or move his eyes; or (d) a person with a perceptual handicap." Singapore's Act largely tracks the categories of beneficiaries in MT but is more restrictive than the MT because Article 3 of the MT also encompasses persons who have a "reading disability."

Second, countries whose national copyright laws already provide exceptions and limitations for the print-disabled must review and, if necessary, revise those laws to ensure that they include all of the different manifestations of disability described in each paragraph of Article 3. For example, Section 32.01 of Canada's Copyright Act defines "print disability" to include the "severe or total impairment of sight"—a phrase that is significantly narrower than the "visual impairment or a perceptual or reading disability" referenced in paragraph (b) of Article 3. Other states' national copyright laws are even more restrictive and will need to be revised when they ratify the MT. For example, Indonesia's copyright statute contains an exception for "reproduction of a scientific, artistic and literary work in Braille for the purposes of the blind," and the Armenian copyright law exempts only "reproduction in Braille, or by other special ways foreseen for the blind."[38] In addition to applying to only one of the three categories of individuals referenced in Article 3, neither law incorporates the flexible, format-neutral approach of MT Article 2(b), discussed above.

Third, states may choose to harmonize laws that implement the MT with laws that implement broader definitions of disability in international agreements or regional legislation. For example, India and Israel (both of which have ratified the Treaty) extend the right to make and share accessible format copies to any disabled person.[39] In addition, the EU Information Society Directive stresses that it is "important for the Member States to adopt all necessary measures to facilitate access to works by persons suffering from a disability which constitutes an obstacle to the use of the works themselves, and to pay particular attention to accessible formats."[40] Article 5.3(b) of the Directive thus authorizes the adoption of copyright exceptions and limitations for "uses, for the benefit of people with a disability, which are directly related to the disability and of a non-commercial nature, to the extent required by the specific disability."[41] In giving effect to this provision, many EU countries have enacted exceptions that benefit individuals with a broad array of physical and mental disabilities.[42]

Nothing in the Marrakesh Treaty requires states to narrow preexisting copyright exceptions that go beyond the minimum requirements of

---

38. Indonesian Copyright Law, art. 15(d); Law on Copyright and Related Rights of 15 June 2006 (Armenia), art. 22(2)(ii).
39. Law for Making Works, Performances and Broadcasts Accessible for Persons with Disabilities (Law Amendments), §1(A), 2014 (Israel), http://www.wipo.int/wipolex/en/text.jsp?file_id=341960; The Copyright (Amendment) Act, § 32, 2012 (India), http://www.wipo.int/wipolex/en/text.jsp?file_id=342028.
40. InfoSoc Directive, *supra* note 7, preamble ¶ 43.
41. *Id.* art. 5(3)(b).
42. For example, Austria's Federal Law on Copyrights on Literary and Artistic Works and Related Rights exempts the reproduction and dissemination of materials for "disabled persons." Federal Law on Copyrights on Literary and Artistic Works and Related Rights, No. 58/2010 (Austria), art. 42d(1). The Irish Copyright and Related Rights Act, 2000 (No. 28 of 2000), arts. 104, 252, identifies the beneficiary of such an exception as "a person who has a physical or mental disability." The copyright law of France defines beneficiaries as "people with one or more disabilities," including disabilities that are "physical, sensory, mental, cognitive or psychological." Law No. 2006-961 of 1 August 2006 on Copyright and Related Rights in the Information Society (France), art. L. 122-5, 7°.

Article 3. Thus, for example, a state that already extends access and sharing rights to individuals with other disabilities is not required to change that law before it can ratify the MT. To the contrary, such retrogressive measures would be incompatible with the MT's overarching human rights objectives. Adopting a broader definition of beneficiary persons is also consistent with the "evolving concept" of disability recognized in the CRPD's Preamble. Moreover, such an approach responds to the practical reality—reflected in Article 3's "regardless of any other disabilities" clause—that many individuals with visual impairments also have other disabilities and experience multiple forms of discrimination.[43]

At the same time, a state that adopts a broader definition of beneficiary persons must ensure that this choice is compatible with the IP treaties it has ratified. The MT does not limit preexisting flexibilities available under these treaties, and the references in MT Article 11 to the three-step test (discussed below) make clear that international IP commitments remain in force. Thus, to the extent that a state broadens the categories of beneficiaries covered by the MT, it will need to justify that choice by reference to other international obligations, including human rights instruments such as the CRPD.

2.5. EXCEPTIONS AND LIMITATIONS TO COPYRIGHT IN NATIONAL LAW

2.5.1. Introduction and Overview

The Marrakesh Treaty requires ratifying countries to introduce in their national laws specific exceptions and limitations (E&Ls) to several exclusive rights of copyright owners. The inclusion of mandatory E&Ls is one of the Treaty's signature achievements. These mandatory provisions are supplemented by certain non-mandatory E&Ls which, if adopted, will increase the availability of accessible format copies and enable states to fully extend MT rights to beneficiary persons and authorized entities. The mandatory and non-mandatory E&Ls are described in Articles 4 through

---

43. *E.g.,* European Union Non-discrimination Law and Intersectionality: Investigating the Triangle of Racial, Gender and Disability Discrimination (Dagmar Schiek & Anna Lawson eds., 2011).

7 of the MT, which constitute the nucleus of the Treaty's substantive provisions, as well as in Articles 11 and 12, which lay down general conditions for the implementation of E&Ls.

This section of the Guide focuses on Article 4, which concerns E&Ls to the exclusive rights of reproduction, distribution, making available to the public, and public performance. Subsequent sections address the cross-border exchange of accessible format copies (Article 5), importation of accessible format copies (Article 6), and technological protection measures (Article 7).

TEXT OF THE MARRAKESH TREATY

Article 4
National Law Limitations and Exceptions Regarding Accessible Format Copies

1. (a) Contracting Parties shall provide in their national copyright laws for a limitation or exception to the right of reproduction, the right of distribution, and the right of making available to the public as provided by the WIPO Copyright Treaty (WCT), to facilitate the availability of works in accessible format copies for beneficiary persons. The limitation or exception provided in national law should permit changes needed to make the work accessible in the alternative format.

   (b) Contracting Parties may also provide a limitation or exception to the right of public performance to facilitate access to works for beneficiary persons.

2. A Contracting Party may fulfill Article 4(1) for all rights identified therein by providing a limitation or exception in its national copyright law such that:

   (a) Authorized entities shall be permitted, without the authorization of the copyright rightholder, to make an accessible format copy of a work, obtain from another authorized entity an accessible format copy, and supply those copies

continued from previous page

> to beneficiary persons by any means, including by non-commercial lending or by electronic communication by wire or wireless means, and undertake any intermediate steps to achieve those objectives, when all of the following conditions are met:
>
> (i) the authorized entity wishing to undertake said activity has lawful access to that work or a copy of that work;
>
> (ii) the work is converted to an accessible format copy, which may include any means needed to navigate information in the accessible format, but does not introduce changes other than those needed to make the work accessible to the beneficiary person;
>
> (iii) such accessible format copies are supplied exclusively to be used by beneficiary persons; and
>
> (iv) the activity is undertaken on a non-profit basis;
>
> and
>
> (b) A beneficiary person, or someone acting on his or her behalf including a primary caretaker or caregiver, may make an accessible format copy of a work for the personal use of the beneficiary person or otherwise may assist the beneficiary person to make and use accessible format copies where the beneficiary person has lawful access to that work or a copy of that work.
>
> 3. A Contracting Party may fulfill Article 4(1) by providing other limitations or exceptions in its national copyright law pursuant to Articles 10 and 11.
>
> 4. A Contracting Party may confine limitations or exceptions under this Article to works which, in the particular accessible format, cannot be obtained commercially under reasonable terms for beneficiary persons in that market. Any Contracting Party availing itself of this possibility shall so declare in a notification deposited with the Director General of WIPO at the time

> *continued from previous page*
>
> of ratification of, acceptance of or accession to this Treaty or at any time thereafter.
> 5. It shall be a matter for national law to determine whether limitations or exceptions under this Article are subject to remuneration.

2.5.2. Obligations of Article 4(1)

2.5.2.1. MANDATORY EXCEPTIONS AND LIMITATIONS

Article 4(1)(a) requires states to introduce E&Ls in their domestic laws "to facilitate the availability of works in accessible format copies for beneficiary persons." Specifically, national laws must incorporate E&Ls to the following exclusive rights of copyright owners: the right of reproduction, the right of distribution, and the right of making available to the public.[44] These E&Ls authorize two types of activities: (1) the creation of accessible format copies; and (2) the transfer of those copies to beneficiary persons, either directly or via an authorized entity. The following table outlines the types of activities that Article 4(1)(a) requires and provides examples of each activity:

Exclusive right	Types of activities authorized	Examples
Reproduction	– Conversion of copies in conventional formats into accessible format copies	– Creation of an audiobook from a conventional book
	– Reproduction of accessible format copies	– Making copies of a Braille book

(*Continued*)

---

44. For additional information about the content and scope of these exclusive rights, see SAM RICKETSON & JANE C. GINSBURG, INTERNATIONAL COPYRIGHT AND NEIGHBOURING RIGHTS: THE BERNE CONVENTION AND BEYOND (2d ed. 2006).

Exclusive right	Types of activities authorized	Examples
Distribution	– Transfer or sale of accessible format copies to or between beneficiary persons, to or between beneficiary persons and authorized entities, or between authorized entities—whether or not through the transfer of ownership	– Non-commercial lending of accessible e-books – Gifts and donations
Making available	– Scanning and uploading files into the "cloud" or other digital storage system for purposes of creating a library of works available for use exclusively by beneficiary persons	– Posting of an audiobook or e-book for download by beneficiaries or authorized entities on a password-protected site, listservs, or other online communities directed solely at serving print-disabled persons

The last sentence of Article 4(1)(a) provides that the E&L "should permit changes needed to make the work accessible in the alternative format." Put simply, this sentence clarifies that Marrakesh Treaty beneficiaries and authorized entities are entitled to modify copyrighted works if necessary to make such works accessible to print-disabled individuals. The E&L adopted in national implementing legislation must therefore permit changes that may constitute derivative works under domestic copyright laws, as well as changes that may interfere with the integrity of a work under Article 6*bis* of the Berne Convention.[45] Such modifications may

---

45. Article 6*bis* provides in relevant part that "the author shall have the right to claim authorship of the work and to object to any distortion, mutilation or other modification of, or other derogatory action in relation to, the said work, which would be prejudicial to his honor or reputation."

include preparing written descriptions of photographs or other art in a book; converting written text into audio, Braille, or other accessible formats; making tactile graphics based on images in a book; or adapting font style or size.

The last sentence of Article 4(1)(a) does not limit the nature or scope of permitted changes; rather, it authorizes any changes necessary to make covered works accessible to beneficiaries. Given the wide array of print disabilities and the differing technological needs of individuals who experience those disabilities, states should fully implement this provision of the Treaty to permit beneficiaries and authorized entities to make whatever modifications are necessary to make a work accessible to all print-disabled persons.

2.5.2.2. NON-MANDATORY EXCEPTIONS AND LIMITATIONS

In addition to the mandatory E&Ls required by Article 4(1)(a), Article 4(1)(b) authorizes (but does not require) states to adopt an E&L to the right of public performance. Such an exception would, for example, permit public recital of literary works for the benefit of the print disabled. To implement the Marrakesh Treaty in ways that better promote its human rights objectives, states should adopt the non-mandatory E&Ls referenced in Article 4. By exercising their discretion to adopt such exceptions, states will more effectively advance the MT's goal of maximizing opportunities for print-disabled individuals to create, use, enjoy, and share covered copyrighted works on terms equivalent to non-print-disabled persons.

2.5.3. Modes of Implementing Article 4(1)

The Marrakesh Treaty gives governments considerable flexibility to give effect to Article 4(1) in their respective national legal systems. The two principal modes of implementation are outlined in Articles 4(2) and 4(3):

2.5.3.1. ARTICLE 4(2)—THE SAFE HARBOR OPTION

Article 4(2) provides a model that states may follow in meeting their obligations under Article 4(1). This model incorporates the requirements of the three-step test (TST), also referenced in Article 11, which requires that the E&Ls enacted to implement Article 4(1) be limited to special cases that do not conflict with a normal exploitation of the work and do not unreasonably prejudice the legitimate interests of the rights holder. Article 4(2) thus creates a "safe harbor" for ratifying states because legislation that follows this suggested approach presumptively meets the requirements of the TST. (We discuss the TST in more detail below in Section 2.8 of the Guide.)

Article 4(2) identifies the E&Ls that national legislation must create as well as the conditions for satisfying the TST. The first part of Article 4(2) describes a recommended E&L for authorized entities; the second part describes a recommended E&L for beneficiary persons. States must enact both provisions in order to comply with the MT.

2.5.3.1.1. The Safe Harbor for Authorized Entities

Under Article 4(2)(a), an acceptable E&L for authorized entities is one that permits authorized entities to engage in three distinct activities:

- making an accessible format copy,
- obtaining such a copy from another authorized entity, and
- supplying the copy directly to a beneficiary person, by any means.

Article 4(2)(a) also provides that national legislation must ensure that copies may be supplied by, among other means, non-commercial lending and "by electronic communication by wire or wireless means." Thus, states must permit distribution and sharing of accessible format copies through the Internet, a library, or other lending system. Finally, Article 4(2) permits authorized entities to "undertake any intermediate steps to achieve those objectives." This may include, for example, making backup copies of a work, as well as storing or archiving such copies, to enable conversion into a variety of different formats in the future.

The introduction of an E&L for authorized entities is subject to four cumulative conditions that seek to balance the rights of beneficiary persons against the interests of copyright holders. These conditions delineate the outer boundaries of the safe harbor E&Ls for authorized entities. States must include all four of these conditions in national implementing legislation:

(i) the authorized entity "has lawful access to that work or a copy thereof;"
(ii) the work is converted into an accessible format, provided the conversion does not introduce changes to the work beyond those that are necessary to make it accessible;
(iii) the accessible format copies "are supplied exclusively to be used by beneficiary persons;" and
(iv) the activity is "undertaken on a non-profit basis."

With regard to the first condition, "lawful access" includes access by purchase or by license, or access obtained pursuant to another E&L in national copyright law. For example, if a library licenses an electronic copy of a book or other literary or artistic work covered by the MT, the library has lawful access to a copy of the work and its staff may make an accessible format version available to beneficiary persons.

2.5.3.1.2. The Safe Harbor for Beneficiary Persons

Article 4(2)(b) also provides a model for adopting an E&L on behalf of beneficiary persons. Under Article 4(2)(b), an acceptable E&L must make it lawful for both a print-disabled individual and someone acting on his or her behalf—such as a caregiver, teacher, or librarian—to make an accessible format copy of a work.

Two cumulative conditions apply to this E&L: the copy must be for the personal use of the beneficiary, and the beneficiary must have "lawful access" to the work or a copy thereof, as explained above. As with the safe harbor for authorized entities, a state that adopts an E&L for beneficiary persons following the template of Article 4(2)(b) will presumptively satisfy the requirements of the TST.

2.5.3.1.3. Implications of the Safe Harbor Options

Following the safe harbor models of Article 4(2) has important consequences for international copyright law and for the settlement of WTO disputes relating to the TRIPS Agreement. In particular, states that follow the multilaterally-sanctioned template in Article 4(2) have a strong argument that domestic implementing legislation that follows that template does not violate TRIPS or other copyright conventions that include the TST. Finding such legislation to be contrary to these IP treaties would be inconsistent with the Marrakesh Treaty's plain language, undermine its object and purpose, and render Article 4(2) devoid of practical meaning. Moreover, the fact that the Treaty *prescribes* a specific model for implementing its core obligations is strong evidence that that model is consistent with international copyright law, including the TST.

In addition to harmonizing the rights and obligations in multiple international legal instruments, following the safe harbor models of Article 4(2) has other benefits. It enhances certainty and predictability concerning the MT's interpretation, it facilitates the exchange of accessible format copies across national borders, and it demonstrates the benefits of such exchanges to other countries, encouraging them to ratify and implement the Treaty.

2.5.3.2. ARTICLE 4(3)—THE SUI GENERIS OPTION

As an alternative to the safe harbor in Article 4(2), Article 4(3) of the Marrakesh Treaty permits a ratifying state to fulfill the obligations in Article 4(1) by providing or relying upon "other" E&Ls in its national law. Countries are thus free to develop their own approach to implementing Article 4(1), for example, by relying on existing statutory exceptions to copyright, including doctrines such as fair use or fair dealing. However, a state that chooses this sui generis approach must ensure that the resulting E&Ls are consistent with other Marrakesh Treaty requirements, including the TST referenced in Article 11 and in other provisions of the Treaty.

Although the sui generis option thus gives governments significant discretion to tailor national implementing legislation to their specific policy goals and the needs of domestic beneficiaries, too much variation between the national laws of countries that ratify the Marrakesh Treaty also has a cost. The more that states harmonize their domestic implementation of the MT, the more they will facilitate cross-border exchanges of accessible format copies. This is especially important for developing and least-developed countries, many of which have limited financial and technological means to create such copies domestically and will need to rely on the copies transferred from developed countries. For this reason, as well as to enhance legal certainty and predictability, states should consider choosing the safe harbor approach over the sui generis option.

2.5.4. Exceptions and Limitations for the Translation of Copyrighted Works

Many copyrighted works are not published in or translated into languages understood by individuals with print disabilities. The availability of such works in local languages is thus a key aspect of ensuring that beneficiary persons fully realize the access and sharing rights provided in the MT. For print-disabled persons in developing and least-developed countries in particular, having an accessible format copy, such as an audiobook, in a language they understand is vital to achieving the Treaty's broader objective of addressing the book famine.

The Agreed Statement to Marrakesh Treaty Article 4(3) clarifies that the enactment of E&Ls pursuant to this provision "neither reduces nor extends the scope of applicability" of E&Ls states may enact to the exclusive right of translation pursuant to the Berne Convention. In other words, the MT affirms both the scope of the translation right recognized in the Berne Convention as well as the preexisting exceptions to that right.[46] States may therefore adopt an exception or limitation that enables beneficiaries and authorized entities to translate a work from one language to another to facilitate access to print-disabled individuals, provided that they do so consistently with the Berne Convention.

2.5.5. The Commercial Availability Option

Article 4(4) of the Marrakesh Treaty allows, but does not require, Contracting Parties to confine the E&Ls adopted pursuant to Article 4 "to works which, in the particular accessible format, cannot be obtained

---

46. As leading commentators on international copyright law have explained, the right of translation has historically been subject to a range of E&Ls in national laws. RICKETSON & GINSBURG, *supra* note 44, § 13.83 (discussing implied exceptions to translation rights).

commercially under reasonable terms for beneficiary persons in that market." Under this "commercial availability option," a state may choose to narrow the reach of the MT by prohibiting the creation of accessible format copies of works that the copyright owner has made commercially available in that particular format. For example, a state may decide that the E&L should not authorize the conversion of an academic textbook into Braille if that textbook has already been published in Braille and is available for purchase from the publisher.

At the outset, it is important to emphasize that the commercial availability option is format specific. States may only exclude works that are already available in the particular format sought by a print-disabled person. The availability of a work in one accessible format (such as Braille) cannot prevent a beneficiary or authorized entity from creating or sharing a copy in a different accessible format (such as an e-book or audiobook). This also furthers the MT's object and purpose, since not all formats are accessible to all beneficiaries.

Although the MT permits ratifying countries to adopt a commercial availability requirement, doing so increases the challenges for and burdens on print-disabled individuals. This Guide therefore recommends that states extend E&Ls to all covered works, including works that are commercially available. Prior to the negotiation of the MT, few countries whose copyright laws included E&Ls for print-disabled individuals included a commercial availability provision. Some countries with such a provision limited it to copies available under reasonable conditions.[47] These differences among countries means there is little guidance as to how such a standard might operate internationally and what impact it would have on the availability of accessible format copies. The unresolved questions relating to the commercial availability requirement include the following:

- What does commercial *availability* entail? Does it require availability in bookstores? Online? Do bookstores carrying the accessible format copy need to be accessible to

---

47. *See* WIPO STUDY, *supra* note 4, at 112–13.

beneficiaries in terms of geographic location and physical accessibility? Should the notion of availability include affordability?
- What does *commercial* mean? Does the work need to be offered by a for-profit entity? Or does "commercial" refer to how widely the accessible copy is offered?
- *When* should availability be assessed? At the time of publication of the work, at the time a print-disabled person seeks to purchase the work, or at some other time?
- *Where* should commercial availability be assessed? Globally? Regionally? In the relevant national market of a print-disabled person?

The absence of settled answers to these questions counsels states to reject the option of restricting E&Ls to accessible format works that are commercially unavailable. Such a restriction would be fundamentally inconsistent with the MT's overarching goal of ensuring that individuals with print disabilities have an equal opportunity to enjoy covered works on the same terms as sighted persons. The restriction also risks restricting the rights that print-disabled individuals have under other copyright E&Ls, such as exceptions for private copying. The lack of clarity about what constitutes commercial availability would also create significant legal risks for authorized entities and beneficiaries that could deter the effective exercise of their rights under the Treaty.

If, notwithstanding these concerns, a Contracting State nevertheless adopts a commercial availability restriction, this decision cannot diminish the ability of authorized entities to exchange works across borders. Article 5 (discussed below) does not provide affirmative authority for limiting exports to works that are commercially unavailable. Thus, as long as the copy was lawfully made in the jurisdiction in which it originates, it may be exported to other Contracting Parties.

2.5.6. *The Remuneration Option*

Article 4(5) of the Marrakesh Treaty permits states to decide whether E&Ls adopted pursuant to Article 4 should be subject to remuneration.

This optional provision allows states to condition the creation, distribution, or making available of accessible format copies upon the payment of a royalty or other license fee to the copyright holder.

Although the option of requiring remuneration is available to states, it should generally be avoided. Article 4(5) ensures that countries that already have a remuneration requirement are not required to change their existing laws. It also gives states discretion to include a remuneration requirement in newly adopted E&Ls.

However, a widely adopted remuneration requirement would impede the creation and exchange of accessible format works in at least two respects. First, it would introduce unnecessary complexity that could deter beneficiaries and authorized entities from exercising their MT rights. Second, remuneration creates a financial burden that may make works effectively unavailable for many print-disabled individuals. Remuneration thus poses a particular risk for developing and least-developed countries, as well as for poor individuals in middle-income and wealthy countries.

A broad remuneration requirement also creates a risk of discrimination between print-disabled and non-print-disabled individuals. The exercise of rights under national E&Ls is not typically conditioned on the payment of compensation, and if required, remuneration generally applies only to specific and narrow statutory licenses.[48] Imposing remuneration for the exercise of MT rights would therefore place a burden on print-disabled individuals that does not generally apply to non-print-disabled individuals. This would not only be inconsistent with the MT's objectives, but could also conflict with a state's obligation to avoid discrimination on the basis of disability as mandated by the CRPD and other international human rights treaties.

States that nonetheless decide to create or retain a remuneration requirement should ensure that it minimizes the burden on print-disabled

---

48. Nor is remuneration required by international human rights law. The Special Rapporteur on Cultural Rights, for example, has explained that uncompensated uses can be consistent with the protection of the interests of authors, particularly where requiring compensation would create a financial or administrative barrier to legitimate uses. *See* SR Copyright Report, *supra* note 3, ¶ 72.

individuals. If the cost of remuneration falls on individual beneficiaries, it must be set at rates that do not make works financially inaccessible and that are appropriate to economic, social, and cultural circumstances in different jurisdictions.

The *process* for settling on the amount of remuneration must also minimize the burden on print-disabled individuals. A statutory scheme that establishes predetermined rates would provide clarity to MT beneficiaries and authorized entities; requiring those actors to negotiate with each copyright owner, in contrast, risks imposing an infeasible administrative burden. If negotiation is required, the state must ensure that beneficiaries and authorized entities can continue to enjoy the rights to make and share accessible format copies prior to reaching an agreement over compensation. In other words, copyright owners should not be allowed to prevent beneficiaries from enjoying their rights under the MT by refusing to negotiate or by setting unreasonably high licensing rates. Finally, the government should continually monitor the remuneration requirement to ensure that is does not impede effective implementation of the Treaty.

2.6. CROSS-BORDER EXCHANGE AND IMPORTATION OF ACCESSIBLE FORMAT COPIES

2.6.1. Introduction and Overview

Articles 5 and 6 of the Marrakesh Treaty regulate the cross-border exchange of accessible format copies. These complementary provisions operate in tandem with Article 4 to enhance the global diffusion of such copies, including by requiring states to permit the export and import of accessible format copies subject to certain conditions. The Treaty seeks to accomplish these objectives by requiring exceptions and limitations to the right of distribution of copyrighted works and the right of making such works available. As with Article 4, although the adoption of these E&Ls is mandatory, the Treaty provides flexibility to states in giving effect to these provisions in legislation implementing the MT or other national laws.

TEXT OF THE MARRAKESH TREATY

<u>Article 5</u>
Cross-Border Exchange of Accessible Format Copies

1. Contracting Parties shall provide that if an accessible format copy is made under a limitation or exception or pursuant to operation of law, that accessible format copy may be distributed or made available by an authorized entity to a beneficiary person or an authorized entity in another Contracting Party.
2. A Contracting Party may fulfill Article 5(1) by providing a limitation or exception in its national copyright law such that:
   (a) authorized entities shall be permitted, without the authorization of the rightholder, to distribute or make available for the exclusive use of beneficiary persons accessible format copies to an authorized entity in another Contracting Party; and
   (b) authorized entities shall be permitted, without the authorization of the rightholder and pursuant to Article 2(c), to distribute or make available accessible format copies to a beneficiary person in another Contracting Party;
   provided that prior to the distribution or making available the originating authorized entity did not know or have reasonable grounds to know that the accessible format copy would be used for other than beneficiary persons.
3. A Contracting Party may fulfill Article 5(1) by providing other limitations or exceptions in its national copyright law pursuant to Articles 5(4), 10 and 11.
4. (a) When an authorized entity in a Contracting Party receives accessible format copies pursuant to Article 5(1) and that Contracting Party does not have obligations under Article 9 of the Berne Convention, it will ensure, consistent with its own legal system and practices, that the accessible format copies are only reproduced, distributed or made available for the benefit of beneficiary persons in that Contracting Party's jurisdiction.

continued from previous page

> (b) The distribution and making available of accessible format copies by an authorized entity pursuant to Article 5(1) shall be limited to that jurisdiction unless the Contracting Party is a Party to the WIPO Copyright Treaty or otherwise limits limitations and exceptions implementing this Treaty to the right of distribution and the right of making available to the public to certain special cases which do not conflict with a normal exploitation of the work and do not unreasonably prejudice the legitimate interests of the rightholder.
> (c) Nothing in this Article affects the determination of what constitutes an act of distribution or an act of making available to the public.
>
> 5. Nothing in this Treaty shall be used to address the issue of exhaustion of rights.
>
> Article 6
> Importation of Accessible Format Copies
>
> To the extent that the national law of a Contracting Party would permit a beneficiary person, someone acting on his or her behalf, or an authorized entity, to make an accessible format copy of a work, the national law of that Contracting Party shall also permit them to import an accessible format copy for the benefit of beneficiary persons, without the authorization of the rightholder.

2.6.2. *Substantive Obligations of Articles 5 and 6*

2.6.2.1. ARTICLE 5—EXPORT OF ACCESSIBLE FORMAT COPIES

Article 5(1) requires states to allow authorized entities within their borders to transfer accessible format copies of covered copyrighted works to authorized entities and beneficiary persons in other Marrakesh Treaty countries. This transfer or export right, which can be exercised by the distribution of physical or electronic copies, does not require the consent or permission of the copyright owner.

Article 5(1) plays an important role in achieving the MT's objectives. First, it addresses the needs of print-disabled individuals in countries with limited financial or technological ability to produce accessible format materials on their own. Without a right to receive copies made abroad, these individuals would enjoy few of the benefits that the MT is designed to achieve. Second, Article 5(1) seeks to increase the exchange and diffusion of these materials between countries and regions at different levels of socioeconomic development, ensuring that countries with limited or no capacity to produce accessible format copies are not excluded from the MT's benefits. Third, such exchanges avoid inefficiency and duplication of investment in the production of accessible format copies by allowing those works to be shared once they are created, rather than requiring that they be recreated in every country.

The right to export in Article 5(1) applies when the accessible format copy is (1) "made under a limitation or exception" or (2) "pursuant to operation of law." With regard to the first clause, states have considerable leeway to provide the authority to make accessible format copies eligible for export. As explained in greater detail below, the simplest way for a state to authorize the creation of an accessible format copy is by enacting a limitation or exception that is tailor-made for this purpose.

The right to export also applies when the accessible format copy is made "pursuant to operation of law." This phrase appears only once in the MT and is undefined. However, because this phrase is identified as an alternative to "a limitation or exception," a reasonable interpretation is that the phrase includes an accessible format copy made pursuant to any provision of domestic law. In other words, the phrase "operation of law" encompasses domestic laws—such as disability rights and non-discrimination statutes or administrative regulations—that authorize schools and other educational institutions to provide accessible format copies to print-disabled individuals. It also includes laws providing similar authorization to libraries, government agencies, and other non-profit institutions.

In addition, the phrase "operation of law" may apply to works that—although technically satisfying internationally-recognized criteria for copyright protection—are statutorily excluded from copyrightable subject matter. The Agreed Statement concerning Article 5(1), which provides that "nothing in this Treaty reduces or extends the scope of exclusive rights under any other treaty," confirms that states retain these preexisting flexibilities. Article 5(1), in turn, makes clear that states must allow accessible format copies created pursuant to this authority to be exchanged across borders.

As discussed above, Article 4 allows Contracting Parties to condition the creation of an accessible format copy on the commercial unavailability of the work in the desired format (although this Guide recommends against adopting such a requirement). This option does not, however, appear in Article 5. It follows from the established principles of treaty interpretation discussed in Chapter 1 that the MT does not provide affirmative authority for such a restriction. The Treaty's human rights objectives further support the conclusion that states should not condition the export of accessible format copies on the commercial unavailability of the particular formatted work in the destination state.

The right to export accessible format works also does not depend on whether the destination state has enacted a commercial unavailability restriction in its domestic law. It is up to the destination state—not the exporting state—to decide under Article 6 (discussed below) whether to limit imports of accessible format copies to works that are not commercially available in that particular format. Governments may not dictate the discretionary policy choices adopted by other MT states in implementing the Treaty. Conditioning export on whether the destination state would allow the copy to be made would be unworkable, and would impermissibly burden the exercise of MT rights as it would effectively require authorized entities to know the law of all the jurisdictions in which beneficiaries might use accessible format works.

2.6.2.2. ARTICLE 6—IMPORT OF ACCESSIBLE FORMAT COPIES

Functioning as a complement to Article 5(1), Article 6 requires states to allow beneficiary persons, someone acting on their behalf, and authorized entities to import accessible format copies for beneficiary persons without the copyright owner's authorization or consent. Two aspects of Article 6 are worth emphasizing—who can import accessible format copies, and the location from which such copies can originate.

As for the first issue, the words "to the extent" in Article 6 link the right of importation to the right to create accessible format copies required by Article 4. A state that allows print-disabled individuals, their agents, and authorized entities to make an accessible format copy must also, therefore, allow those same actors to import such a copy pursuant to Article 6. Stated more plainly: the right to create carries with it the right to import.

Second, Article 6 does not require that the imported copy originate in a Contracting Party. As a result, countries that have ratified the Treaty may permit importation of accessible format copies from countries that have not ratified the MT. Authorizing importation from these non-MT countries will expand the availability of accessible format copies to print-disabled individuals and authorized entities, wherever they are located.

2.6.3. Modes of Implementation of Articles 5 and 6

As is the case with Article 4, the MT gives governments significant leeway in how they choose to implement Article 5(1) and 6. A summary of the available implementation options follows:

2.6.3.1. ARTICLE 5(2)—THE SAFE HARBOR OPTION

As with Article 4(2), Article 5(2) sets out a method for implementing Article 5(1) that is presumptively compliant with the TST and thus provides a "safe harbor" for MT countries. Specifically, Article 5(2) allows states to implement Article 5(1) by introducing an exception or limitation in their domestic laws that permits authorized entities to distribute or make available accessible format copies to authorized entities or beneficiary persons in another MT country.

States must make this exception or limitation subject to the following two conditions: (1) if the recipient is an authorized entity, the distribution or making available is for the exclusive use of beneficiary persons; and (2) the sending authorized entity, prior to the transfer, does not "know or have reasonable grounds to know that the accessible format copy would be used for other than beneficiary persons." The Agreed Statement to Article 5(2) provides that "it may be appropriate for an authorized entity to apply further measures to confirm that the person it is serving is a beneficiary person and to follow its own practices as described in Article 2(c)." Viewed together, Article 5(2) and its Agreed Statement thus strike a careful balance between ensuring that authorized entities are not subject to burdensome requirements or standards, and ensuring that specific transfers of accessible format copies are made in accordance with the conditions set forth in the MT.[49]

The Agreed Statement also clarifies that states may not impose additional record-keeping or other administrative burdens on authorized entities. These entities may voluntarily employ further measures to confirm that the individuals whom they serve are beneficiaries. The state cannot, however, require authorized entities to engage in these additional measures. This is confirmed by the Agreed Statement's reference to Article 2(c), which explicitly allows authorized entities to follow their own practices in determining whether the individuals they serve are beneficiaries. Requiring additional measures would risk burdening authorized entities and inhibiting them from sharing copies across borders, thus limiting the effectiveness of the Treaty.

2.6.3.2. ARTICLE 5(3)—THE SUI GENERIS OPTION

As an alternative to the "safe harbor" in Article 5(2), Article 5(3) of the Marrakesh Treaty allows ratifying countries to satisfy the export

---

49. A few countries have imposed restrictions on exports that go beyond the Marrakesh Treaty's requirements. Israel, for example, appears to require that an authorized entity satisfy itself that the exported copy will not be transferred or used by non-beneficiary persons. Singapore requires that an exporting authorized entity take steps "prescribed in regulations" to verify the identity of the foreign entity or beneficiary person requesting the materials. Because the precise meaning of these provisions is uncertain, they may deter authorized entities from exporting copies even when doing so would be lawful. More importantly, these provisions are incompatible with the MT to the extent that they charge authorized entities with constructive knowledge that exported copies will be used by non-beneficiary persons.

obligation in Article 5(1) by introducing "other" E&Ls in their domestic laws. In order to enable authorized entities to know what materials they are allowed to export, such laws should clearly define the conditions under which exports are authorized. In addition, E&Ls adopted pursuant to this sui generis option must comply with the requirements of Article 5(4), Article 10 (general principles on implementation), and Article 11 (the three-step test).

Article 5(4) addresses situations in which a country that ratifies the Marrakesh Treaty is not also a party to an IP treaty that requires that state to comply with the three-step test (TST). In such a situation, it is possible that an authorized entity might distribute the work unencumbered by the obligation of the TST. Article 5(4) addresses this by providing that an authorized entity in a state that is not a party to the Berne Convention or the WIPO Copyright Treaty (WCT), or which does not otherwise incorporate the TST in its domestic law, can receive an accessible format copy made in another state but may not distribute that copy to another jurisdiction.

To be more precise, Article 5(4) puts a jurisdictional limitation on the use of accessible format copies that are exported to authorized entities in countries not bound by the TST:

1. Article 5(4)(a). An authorized entity located in a country that is not a party to the Berne Convention that receives an accessible format copy must ensure that such copy is "only reproduced, distributed or made available for the benefit of beneficiary persons *in that Contracting Party's jurisdiction*" (emphasis added).
2. Article 5(4)(b). An authorized entity located in a state that is neither a party to the WCT, nor limits E&Ls enacted to implement the Marrakesh Treaty in ways that comply with the three-step test, must confine any distribution and making available of accessible format copies "to that jurisdiction."

In other words, unless a Contracting Party to the Marrakesh Treaty has also ratified the WCT, or unless its exceptions and limitations are three-step-test compliant, authorized entities located in that state may receive accessible format copies from abroad and may use and distribute such copies domestically, but may not export those copies to another Contracting Party.[50]

Several other conclusions follow from Article 5(4). First, a MT Contracting Party that is *also* a WCT Member is eligible to permit exports of accessible format copies.

Second, a MT Contracting Party that is *not* a WCT Member but which implements exceptions and limitations following the template provided in Article 4(2)—the "safe harbor" implementation approach that presumptively satisfies the TST—may also permit exports of accessible format copies.

Third, a MT Contracting Party that *is not* a WCT member and implements the Marrakesh Treaty by providing or relying on other exceptions and limitations in its domestic law—the *sui generis* approach authorized by Articles 4(3) and 5(3) of the MT—must ensure that these domestic E&Ls are consistent with the TST before permitting exports of accessible format copies.

2.6.4. *Exhaustion of Rights*

Article 5(5) stipulates that the Marrakesh Treaty does not affect the "exhaustion of rights." The exhaustion principle—also known as the "first-sale doctrine"—provides that once the owner of a particular copy of a work sells or transfers ownership to another person or entity *with the authorization of the copyright owner*, the new owner is free to dispose of that copy in any way he or she deems appropriate, including through resale, donation, or lending. Given that Article 5 and the MT as a whole address transfers that are *not authorized by rights holders*, it may seem unnecessary to include a provision on exhaustion in the Treaty. However, similar provisions appear in many other IP conventions. The primary purpose of

---

50. The Agreed Statement to Article 5(4)(b) clarifies that the MT does not require Contracting Parties to either: (1) "apply the three-step test beyond its obligations under this [Treaty] or under other international treaties"; or (2) "ratify or accede to the WCT or to comply with any of its provisions."

these clauses is to emphasize that nothing in those agreements—or in the MT—modifies preexisting international rules concerning exhaustion.

2.6.5. Implementation of Article 6

The Agreed Statement concerning Article 6 specifies that Marrakesh Treaty ratifying countries "have the same flexibilities set out in Article 4 when implementing their obligations under Article 6." This means that all of the options and discretionary choices available when implementing Article 4 are equally applicable to the implementation of Article 6. These "flexibilities" include:

- Article 4(3) allows states to "fulfill Article 4(1) by providing other limitations or exceptions in its national copyright law pursuant to Articles 10 and 11." This flexibility allows states to implement Article 6 through the introduction of other E&Ls, subject to their compliance with the TST.
- Article 4(4) permits states to confine Article 4 E&Ls "to works which, in the particular accessible format, *cannot be obtained commercially* under reasonable terms for beneficiary persons in that market" (emphasis added). Accordingly, each state is permitted—but not required—to introduce a "commercial availability" requirement on imports of accessible format copies.
- Article 4(5) permits states to determine whether Article 4 E&Ls should be made "subject to remuneration." States thus have the discretion to require that imports of accessible format copies be conditioned on payment of a reasonable royalty to the rights holder.

For reasons discussed in the Guide's analysis of MT Article 4, a state that adopts the commercial availability option or the remuneration option risks imposing additional hurdles to the creation and cross-border transfer of accessible format copies. Such impediments undermine the MT's human rights objectives. The negative effects of adopting either provision in the context of Article 6 would be especially severe for beneficiary persons in developing and least-developed countries, many of which have neither the technological capacity nor the financial means to meet the needs of their print-disabled citizens.

2.6.6. Cross-Border Issues Not Addressed in the Marrakesh Treaty

The MT does not address two issues of great importance for expanding the global availability of accessible format copies. States nevertheless have the discretion to regulate these issues, and doing so would enhance the achievement of the Treaty's objectives:

- <u>Distribution of accessible format copies to non-MT countries</u>. Expanding the exchange of accessible format copies to include exports to and imports from countries that are not members of the MT is neither expressly authorized nor expressly prohibited by the Treaty. However, such an expansion offers significant advantages for beneficiary persons worldwide. First, it would make greater numbers and varieties of accessible format copies available to more people with print disabilities in more countries, thus augmenting the Treaty's effects in MT Contracting Parties. Second, it would demonstrate the benefits of cross-border exchanges.

- <u>Direct exchanges between beneficiary persons</u>. Although also not expressly allowed or prohibited by the Treaty, transfers of accessible format copies among print-disabled individuals, including in-person exchanges, sharing via online platforms, and transfers among diaspora communities who share a language, would also help to advance the attainment of the Treaty's goals. Direct exchanges between sighted persons are usually effectuated under one of several exceptions in national copyright law, including personal use, fair use, and exhaustion of rights. Similarly, direct exchanges between beneficiary persons should be contemplated either within these exceptions or explicitly recognized in MT-implementing legislation.

In conclusion, the Marrakesh Treaty's cross-border exchange provisions are central to the effective implementation and operation of the Treaty. Working in tandem with the E&Ls required by Article 4, the export and import rights mandated by Articles 5 and 6 aim to establish a global network for diffusing accessible format copies across borders and increasing the availability of such works to all print-disabled individuals without regard to the financial or technological capacity of the countries in which they reside.

2.7. TECHNOLOGICAL PROTECTION MEASURES

2.7.1. Introduction and Overview

Prohibitions on the circumvention of technological protection measures (TPMs)[51] have been a requirement of international copyright law since the conclusion of the WIPO Copyright Treaty (WCT) and the WIPO Performances and Phonograms Treaty (WPPT) in 1996.[52] Provisions prohibiting the circumvention of TPMs have been incorporated into the national laws of many WIPO member states and in regional and plurilateral trade agreements. As a result, the use of diverse technological tools, often supplemented by restrictive contractual stipulations, has become a standard way that copyright owners regulate access to, and use of, digital works.

However, TPMs can prevent lawful uses of copyrighted works, including accessing, creating, and sharing of accessible format copies by

---

51. "TPMs take various forms and their features are continually changing, but some major features remain constant. The most basic and most important kind of TPM is access control technology. One common way of controlling access is encrypting or scrambling the content. In such case the user gets the data but must follow an additional procedure to make it usable. Another form of access control is a procedure that allows access to a source only with proof of authorisation, for example, password protection . . . . The other major type of TPM, copy or use controls, enable the rights owner to allow certain permitted activities but to prevent illicit activities by a user who has access to the work." IFPI, *The WIPO Treaties: Technological Measures* (2003), http://www.ifpi.org/content/library/wipo-treaties-technical-measures.pdf.
52. *See* WCT, art. 11; WPPT, art. 18. A provision requiring the effective legal protection of TPMs also appears in Article 15 of the 2012 Beijing Treaty on Audiovisual Performances.

print-disabled persons and authorized entities. Such uses of TPMs can impede the exercise and enjoyment of the rights granted in the Marrakesh Treaty and frustrate the objectives of the CRPD because TPMs impose barriers on disabled individuals that prevent them from fully participating in society. The MT aims to strike a balance between upholding legal rules that prevent the circumvention of TPMs while ensuring that such rules do not deter or impede print-disabled individuals and authorized entities from accessing, creating, and sharing accessible format copies. These issues are addressed in Article 7 of the Treaty.

TEXT OF THE MARRAKESH TREATY

Article 7

Obligations Concerning Technological Measures

Contracting Parties shall take appropriate measures, as necessary, to ensure that when they provide adequate legal protection and effective legal remedies against the circumvention of effective technological measures, this legal protection does not prevent beneficiary persons from enjoying the limitations and exceptions provided for in this Treaty.

2.7.2. Analysis

Article 7 requires states that provide legal protection of TPMs to ensure that such protection does not prevent the exercise of the E&Ls required by Article 4, or the rights conferred under Articles 5 and 6 of the Treaty. The exceptions required by the MT are in addition to any existing or future exceptions to TPMs provided under national law. Under Article 7, states must ensure that exceptions to the legal protection of TPMs exist for individuals with print disabilities and for authorized entities. Accordingly, where national law prohibits the circumvention of TPMs, a state must ensure that this prohibition prevents neither the creation of nor access to digital works, nor their legitimate sharing and use by authorized entities and beneficiary persons.

Several interrelated principles can be gleaned from the text of Article 7. First, states that do protect TPMs must ensure that the rights of MT beneficiaries and authorized entities are not impaired by such protection, either formally (for example, in legislation or administrative regulations) or in practice (for example, due to the actions of copyright owners or other private actors). Article 7 uses the words "shall" and "ensure" to underscore the mandatory nature of this obligation to safeguard the rights of print-disabled persons against uses of TPMs that interfere with MT rights—an emphasis that is required by the MT's human rights goals.

Second, Article 7 only applies to MT states that prohibit the circumvention of TPMs. A number of countries do not currently have an international obligation to enact such a prohibition, such as those not parties to the WCT or WPPT. Although Article 7 does not formally apply to these states unless and until they enact laws prohibiting the circumvention of TPMs, it is nonetheless recommended that such states include in legislation implementing the MT an exemption from anti-circumvention laws for the creation and sharing of accessible format copies by authorized entities and beneficiaries. This will ensure that authorized entities and beneficiaries are protected if the state does later adopt legislation prohibiting the circumvention of TPMs, or in cases where private contractual arrangements prohibiting circumvention have a similar effects on MT rights.

Third, the simplest and least burdensome way to implement Article 7 is by enacting a legislative or administrative exemption to the ban on circumventing TPMs. For example, the U.S. Library of Congress (in which the U.S. Copyright Office is located) is empowered to exempt works from the prohibition on circumventing TPMs. Since 2003, it has exempted literary works in electronic form for the use of individuals with disabilities.[53] Although the Library of Congress process has shortcomings (discussed below), its express exemption sends a clear signal to beneficiaries and authorized entities that they can circumvent TPMs to create accessible format copies.

Without such an express exemption, beneficiaries and authorized entities would have to assert MT-based or other copyright E&Ls as defenses

---

53. For the current version of the regulation, see Exemptions to Prohibition against Circumvention, 37 C.F.R. § 201.40(b)(2) (2015).

in a lawsuit, and the associated legal risk might cause some to refrain from exercising MT rights. The experience of European Union member states has also shown that relying on courts or administrative agencies to resolve conflicts between copyright E&Ls and TPMs has not been effective in protecting the exercise of lawful rights.[54] An express legislative or administrative exemption best achieves the object and purpose of the MT in general, and of Articles 4 and 7 in particular.

Any such exemption should also be both permanent and technology neutral. For example, the U.S. Library of Congress, which requires the exemption to be renewed periodically, subjects beneficiaries to the vagaries of the administrative rule-making process. The earliest versions of the exemption were also limited to "[l]iterary works distributed in ebook format when all existing ebook editions of the work (including digital text editions made available by authorized entities) contain access controls that prevent the enabling of the ebook's read-aloud function and that prevent the enabling of screen readers to render the text into a specialized format."[55] Such a limitation was in tension with the CRPD because it was confined to specific assistive technologies that some print-disabled individuals may not have been able to use or that may not have responded to their needs. The exemption was revised in 2012 to eliminate references to particular formats and to focus on functionality.

A technologically neutral approach better fulfills the purposes of the MT because it allows beneficiaries and authorized entities to engage in any activity necessary to make a work accessible regardless of TPMs. Such an approach would also be consistent with the definition of "accessible format copy" in MT Article 2(b) as a copy that permits print-disabled individuals "to have access as feasibly and comfortably as a person without visual impairment or other print disability."

---

54. The EU InfoSoc Directive requires states to ensure that TPMs do not restrict the exercise of copyright exceptions. InfoSoc Directive, *supra* note 7, ¶¶ 51–52. Notwithstanding this requirement, many EU member states have not included a provision in their respective national laws exempting circumvention of TPMs to ensure access, whereas others have included only a general statement about the importance of avoiding conflict or have delegated the matter to a court or agency. None of these approaches have proven effective in ensuring that TPMs do not inhibit lawful access. Caterina Sganga, *Disability, Right to Culture and Copyright: Which Regulatory Option?*, 29 INT'L REV. LAW, COMPUTERS & TECH. 88, 102 (2015).
55. *See, e.g.,* 37 C.F.R. § 201.40(b)(4) (2003).

Other approaches to complying with Article 7 risk incompatibility with the Marrakesh Treaty's object and purpose. For example, requiring copyright owners to provide authorized entities and beneficiaries with the means to open the "digital lock" created by a TPM risks chilling the exercise of MT rights by placing the onus on beneficiaries and authorized entities to affirmatively request access on a work-by-work basis.

Even creating an express exemption still puts a burden on beneficiaries and authorized entities to take affirmative measures to circumvent a TPM, thus denying individuals with print disabilities access to printed materials on a basis of equality with others. Beneficiaries and authorized entities may lack the technical capacity to circumvent TPMs, or they may be fearful that circumvention—even if allowed—creates a risk of civil liability or even criminal punishment. As explained above, the MT itself emphasizes that print-disabled individuals are entitled to access "as feasibly and comfortably" as someone without a print disability. Access that is possible only if one has the requisite know-how, technology, and risk tolerance needed to break a technological lock is not equivalent to the access enjoyed by non-print-disabled individuals.

To alleviate these burdens, states may consider requiring copyright owners to deposit with a library or government agency copies of works without TPMs so that such copies could be provided to beneficiary persons and authorized entities upon request. This approach would help reduce the chilling effect of TPMs by giving beneficiaries and authorized entities access to the deposited version of a work that does not require circumvention. Providing access to such a depository, however, should be in addition to, not instead of, allowing authorized entities and beneficiaries to circumvent TPMs and make accessible format copies on their own.

Finally, the Marrakesh Treaty does not require authorized entities to apply TPMs to accessible format copies; the Agreed Statement to Article 7 merely permits such entities to do so.[56] Inasmuch as ensuring the effective implementation and operation of the Treaty is ultimately the legal responsibility of governments, states must prevent private parties,

---

56. The Agreed Statement on Article 7 provides: "It is understood that authorized entities, in various circumstances, choose to apply technological measures in the making, distribution and making available of accessible format copies and nothing herein disturbs such practices when in accordance with national law."

including authorized entities, from using TPMs to frustrate the realization of these goals.

In sum, the essential purpose of Article 7 is to ensure that TPMs do not impede enjoyment of the rights guaranteed by the Treaty. Avoiding this result is especially important for beneficiaries in developing and least-developed countries, who are likely to be unduly burdened by TPMs. Given that cross-border exchanges of accessible format copies will significantly enhance the social welfare and human rights of print-disabled individuals in some of the world's poorest regions, governments should adopt measures to facilitate the conditions needed for these individuals to effectively enjoy the rights conferred by the MT. Such measures may include, for example, providing exemptions from criminal liability and affirmatively encouraging the development of circumvention technologies available to authorized entities and print-disabled individuals.

2.8. THE THREE-STEP TEST

The three-step test (TST) found in multiple IP treaties appears in several provisions of the Marrakesh Treaty. The first reference occurs in Article 5(4)(b), which limits the distribution and making available of accessible format copies to countries whose E&Ls benefitting print-disabled individuals are either (1) expressly subject to the test, or (2) indirectly subject to it by virtue of the state's membership in the WCT. Article 11, in turn, requires application of the TST when Contracting Parties "adopt[ ] measures necessary to ensure the application of this Treaty."[57]

This section of the Guide explains the policy rationales underlying the TST and the long-standing recognition that E&Ls benefitting the blind are consistent with the test. After describing how this well-settled position informs the proper interpretation of the TST in the MT, the section

---

57. More specifically, Article 11 requires application of the TST as set out in Article 9(2) of the Berne Convention, in Article 13 of the TRIPS Agreement, and in Articles 10(1) and 10(2) of the WCT. Each of the four paragraphs in Article 11 refers to the TST as embodied in these IP treaties. The Marrakesh Treaty's multiple references to different iterations of the TST refer to essentially the same substantive standard. Accordingly, this Guide applies a common interpretation of the TST to all Treaty provisions that reference the test.

concludes that the "safe harbor" E&Ls in Articles 4, 5, and 6 are presumptively compatible with the TST.

2.8.1. Policy Rationales of the Three-Step Test

The TST for evaluating exceptions and limitations has been part of international copyright law for nearly half a century. It was first adopted in connection with the codification of the exclusive right to reproduce copyrighted works, which was introduced in the 1967 Stockholm Revision to the Berne Convention. Article 9(2) of the Berne Convention specified that E&Ls permitting the reproduction of works without the authorization of the copyright holder would be allowed upon satisfaction of three conditions—namely, that such reproduction applies to (1) "certain special cases" that (2) do "not conflict with a normal exploitation of the work" and (3) do "not unreasonably prejudice the legitimate interests of the author."

Since the adoption of the TRIPS Agreement in 1994, the TST has applied to all of the exclusive rights of copyright holders. The WIPO Copyright Treaty of 1996 extended the test to E&Ls to exclusive rights in the digital environment. The TST is thus firmly anchored in international copyright law, a fact that explains its numerous references in the Marrakesh Treaty.

The TST demarcates the policy spaces within which states may legitimately enact E&Ls to the exclusive rights of copyright holders.[58] In this capacity, the test serves a dual purpose. One objective is to safeguard these rights against unduly expansive and unregulated national limitations or exceptions. A second and equally important goal, however, is to prevent "encroach[ment] upon the margin of freedom which the member countries regard[] as indispensable to satisfy important social or cultural needs."[59] E&Ls that are consistent with the TST are thus not merely permissible

---

58. See, e.g., MARTIN SENFTLEBEN, COPYRIGHT, LIMITATIONS AND THE THREE-STEP TEST: AN ANALYSIS OF THE THREE-STEP TEST IN INTERNATIONAL AND EC COPYRIGHT LAW 1 (2004) (stating that when "[v]iewed from a functional perspective," the TST "sets limits to limitations on exclusive rights").

59. Id. at 48.

restrictions on copyright; they are affirmative expressions of government policy that embody socially desirable and salutary objectives, including the realization of a range of internationally protected human rights.[60]

2.8.2. The Three-Step Test and Exceptions and Limitations for the Blind

Despite its functional importance, the TST has been criticized as vague and ambiguous and thus open to a range of interpretations. For example, although some interpretations of the TST view it as cumulative, such that each step of the test must be satisfied for an E&L to be permissible, others disagree.[61] In practice, the TST's application to actual or potential E&Ls has remained unsettled and contested. Few national courts or international tribunals have interpreted the test in the context of concrete disputes involving domestic copyright laws, and commentators remain divided over how to interpret the handful of decisions that have addressed the test.[62]

In light of this ambiguity, the drafting history of the 1967 Revision of the Berne Convention is especially useful for identifying those E&Ls that the Berne negotiators expressly discussed and approved. Of critical importance for the MT, the drafting history clearly demonstrates that E&Ls benefitting the blind have been understood to satisfy the TST since its inception.

A review of the negotiating record reveals that Berne member states agreed in Stockholm to a compromise package deal that codified the exclusive reproduction right in exchange for delineating a common outer

---

60. *See, e.g.*, SR Copyright Report, *supra* note 3, ¶ 61 ("Copyright exceptions and limitations—defining specific uses that do not require a license from the copyright holder—constitute a vital part of the balance that copyright law must strike between the interests of rightsholders in exclusive control and the interests of others in cultural participation.").
61. *See* SENFTLEBEN, *supra* note 58, at 125–27; Max Planck Institute for Innovation and Competition, *A Balanced Interpretation of the "Three-Step Test" in Copyright Law* (Sept. 1, 2008), http://www.ip.mpg.de/en/the-institute/events/patentrechtszyklus.html.
62. *See United States—Section 110(5) of the U.S. Copyright Act*, WTO Doc. WT/DS160/R (June 15, 2000) [hereinafter WTO § 110(5) Panel Report]. *See generally* GRAEME B. DINWOODIE & ROCHELLE C. DREYFUSS, A NEOFEDERALIST VISION OF TRIPS: THE RESILIENCE OF THE INTERNATIONAL INTELLECTUAL PROPERTY REGIME (2012).

boundary to the member states' authority to enact E&Ls to that right in their domestic copyright laws.[63] As part of this compromise, the drafters explicitly recognized that certain long-standing E&Ls were understood to presumptively satisfy the TST. To this end, WIPO prepared a list of E&Ls as they existed in 1967. Berne member states understood this list to constitute "certain special cases" consistent with the TST. Notably, the list specifically referenced two provisions benefitting print-disabled individuals:

> (9) Reproductions in special characters for the use of the blind; [and]
> (10) Sound recordings of literary works for the use of the blind.[64]

Thus, the validity of E&Ls benefitting the blind has been accepted since the initial adoption of the TST in 1967. This recognition has not been questioned in the ensuing five decades, even as international copyright agreements have proliferated. To the contrary, WIPO member states convened a diplomatic conference to adopt the MT for the precise purpose of clarifying and expanding these mandatory E&Ls. This reveals the importance that governments attach to enhancing the ability of persons with print disabilities to access books and other covered works.

2.8.3. Applying the Three-Step Test to the Marrakesh Treaty

The historical importance of E&Ls for the blind—and the understanding that such laws are presumptively compatible with the TST—are important guideposts for interpreting the MT. These long-accepted positions, when viewed in light of the Treaty's overarching objective of making accessible format copies more widely available to print-disabled individuals, yields four distinct conclusions.

Safe Harbor. As explained elsewhere in this Guide, the core obligations in Articles 4, 5, and 6 of the MT provide "safe harbor" options for

---

63. *See* SENFTLEBEN, *supra* note 58, at 81–82.
64. Doc. S/1, Records 1967, at 112, n.1 (cited in SENFTLEBEN, *supra* note 58, at 48).

E&Ls that allow beneficiary persons and authorized entities to create, share, and exchange accessible format copies across borders. A state that takes advantage of these safe harbors and enacts domestic E&Ls that follow the approach set forth in the Treaty should be deemed fully compliant with the TST. In particular, countries need not require compensation or limit MT exceptions to works that are commercially unavailable in order to comply with the TST.

Stated differently, the Marrakesh Treaty's carefully negotiated text updates and expands the permissibility of preexisting E&Ls that benefit individuals with print disabilities. Just as the drafters of the 1967 Revision of the Berne Convention expressly identified national E&Ls for the blind as compatible with the TST, so too the negotiators of the MT unequivocally identified a presumptively legal pathway for states to implement the Treaty's core obligations. Any other interpretation would undermine this carefully crafted multilateral bargain and defeat the Treaty's object and purpose.

Flexible Interpretation of the Three-Step Test. The inclusion of the TST in the MT affirms that the test is flexible enough to encompass other E&Ls outside of the safe harbor. The Marrakesh Treaty itself expressly recognizes in Articles 4(3) and 5(3) that states may fulfill their obligations by providing other E&Ls. The "flexibility" of the test for this purpose is underscored in the Treaty's Preamble,[65] and further reinforced by the references in MT Article 11 to Articles 10(1) and 10(2) of the WCT. Those provisions of the WCT, in turn, must be understood in light of their associated Agreed Statement, which confirms the flexibility of the TST as consistent with national authority to create and maintain E&Ls.[66] Taken together, these references to the WCT, as well as the provisions of the Marrakesh Treaty

---

65. The tenth paragraph of the MT's Preamble reaffirms "the importance and flexibility of the three-step test for limitations and exceptions established in Article 9(2) of the Berne Convention for the Protection of Literary and Artistic Works and other international instruments."
66. The Agreed Statement to Article 10 of the WCT provides: "It is understood that the provisions of Article 10 permit Contracting Parties to carry forward and appropriately extend into the digital environment limitations and exceptions in their national laws which have been considered acceptable under the Berne Convention. Similarly, these provisions should be understood to permit Contracting Parties to devise new exceptions and limitations that

that incorporate the TST, preserve the discretion of governments to devise their own E&Ls to accomplish the Treaty's objectives.

Application in the Digital Environment. The Marrakesh Treaty's extension of E&Ls to copyrighted works in the digital environment is built on the commitment in the WCT Article 10 Agreed Statement, which envisions the extension of E&Ls appropriate to the digital environment. For example, Article 4(1)(a) of the MT directly invokes the "making available" right of the WCT, and Article 4(2)(a) allows authorized entities to supply accessible format copies to beneficiary persons by "any means, including ... by electronic communication by wire or wireless means." Moreover, MT Article 2 defines "works" to include works "in any media." Taken together, these provisions authorize states to adopt E&Ls that enable print-disabled persons and authorized entities to make and share accessible format copies using the full panoply of social media and digital technologies.

Remuneration. The drafting history of the 1967 Stockholm Revision reveals that states have considerable leeway to choose whether or not to require the payment of remuneration to copyright owners with respect to E&Ls that are consistent with the Berne Convention. Uncompensated exceptions—whether for private copying, libraries, quotation, or to serve the interests of the blind—are common in national law. Subsequent case law and commentary have recognized, however, that compensation may in some cases ease the tensions between positive law and normative considerations when applying the third and final step of the TST.[67]

Article 4(5) of the Marrakesh Treaty expressly leaves the choice of whether to provide compensation to each government's discretion. Article 4(5) provides that "*[i]t shall be a matter for national law* to determine whether limitations or exceptions under this Article are subject to remuneration" (emphasis added). If the choice is "a matter for national

---

are appropriate in the digital network environment. It is also understood that Article 10(2) neither reduces nor extends the scope of applicability of the limitations and exceptions permitted by the Berne Convention." WCT, Agreed Statement Concerning Article 10.

67. *See* SENFTLEBEN, *supra* note 58, at 131; *cf.* WTO § 110(5) Panel Report, *supra* note 62, ¶ 6.229.

law," then that choice cannot be foreclosed by international copyright rules—just as exclusions in the Berne Convention that are "a matter for national law" are per se permissible under that treaty.[68] As a result, a MT state that elects not to require compensation when implementing Article 4 cannot—for that reason alone—violate the TST. A contrary interpretation would not only be at odds with the absence of a compensation requirement in many existing national E&Ls that benefit print-disabled individuals, it would also mean that a discretionary decision that the Treaty expressly delegates to governments is not in fact a choice at all.

Commercial Availability. As previously explained, Article 4(4) of the MT gives countries the option of restricting E&Ls to works in formats that beneficiary persons cannot obtain on commercially reasonable terms. For the reasons discussed elsewhere in this Guide, Contracting Parties should refrain from adopting this condition, which may undermine the Treaty's important human rights objectives. Moreover, requiring commercial unavailability does not provide legal security that a state's E&Ls are consistent with international copyright law. To the contrary, as the Agreed Statement to Article 4(4) explains, such a requirement "does not prejudge whether or not a limitation or exception under [Article 4] is consistent with the three-step test."

2.8.4. The Three-Step Test and International Human Rights Law

A flexible application of the TST is also reinforced by international human rights law. As noted in Chapter 1 of this Guide, Article 30(3) of the CRPD obligates states to "take all appropriate steps, in accordance with international law, to ensure that laws protecting intellectual property rights do not constitute an unreasonable or discriminatory barrier to access by persons with disabilities to cultural materials." The CRPD thus implicitly

---

68. For example, Article 2(4) of the Berne Convention provides that "[i]t shall be a matter for legislation in the countries of the Union to determine the protection to be granted to official texts of a legislative, administrative and legal nature, and to official translations of such texts."

reinforces the validity of the long-standing E&Ls favoring the print disabled, and expressly mandates affirmative steps—including a flexible approach to the TST—to mitigate tensions between the exclusive rights of copyright owners and the needs of Marrakesh Treaty beneficiaries.

The inclusion of the TST in the Treaty also illustrates a possible role that the test may play in an IP system that respects human rights. As the Special Rapporteur on Culture recently explained, "[s]tates have a positive obligation to provide for a robust and flexible system of copyright exceptions and limitations to honour their human rights obligations. The 'three-step test' of international copyright law should be interpreted to encourage the establishment of such a system of exceptions and limitations."[69] This statement sees the TST as mediating between the two legal regimes, ensuring states can apply copyright law in ways that protect human rights and guard against abuses by copyright holders.

---

69. SR Copyright Report, *supra* note 3, ¶ 104.

Chapter 3

Putting the Marrakesh Treaty into Practice in National Law

It is essential that the overarching human rights objective of the Marrakesh Treaty—to increase the availability of accessible format copies to print-disabled individuals—is realized not only on paper but also in practice. Article 10(1) of the MT reflects this commitment, emphasizing that each state must "adopt the measures necessary to ensure the application of this Treaty."

Effective implementation of the MT need not be expensive or complicated, however. At the most basic level, each ratifying country must revise its national copyright laws to authorize the making, using, and sharing of accessible format copies. However, to fully realize the MT's objectives, states should also build on their preexisting implementation of human rights treaties, including, in particular, the CRPD. Responsibility for putting the MT into practice may also be entrusted to government IP agencies or offices, working in partnership with human rights institutions.

The sections that follow explain how states can achieve effective implementation by creating legal remedies that allow beneficiaries and authorized entities to assert their rights to create and share accessible format copies (3.1); by vesting authority over the MT in appropriate domestic human rights and IP institutions (3.2); and by authorizing these institutions to engage in monitoring and enforcement activities (3.3).

3.1. CREATE LEGAL REMEDIES

Incorporating the MT into national law is a necessary, but not a sufficient step to ensure the rights of print-disabled persons to make and share accessible format copies. States must also provide remedies for violations of these rights. Access to a remedy is an important principle of international human rights law. It is also critical to ensuring that the rights in the MT are effective in practice. Access to a remedy means that print-disabled individuals and authorized entities must have a means of complaining if the law does not adequately meet their needs or if third parties violate their rights.

States can provide access to remedies by ensuring that individuals with print disabilities, their representative organizations, and authorized entities can assert the right to create and share accessible format copies as defenses in judicial proceedings. For example, in *HathiTrust*, a recent U.S. lawsuit against libraries that digitized books to enable access by print-disabled individuals, the libraries successfully asserted defenses to claims of copyright infringement under both fair use and the Chafee Amendment—specialized legislation in the U.S. that creates exceptions to copyright for activities on behalf of print-disabled individuals.[70]

States should also ensure that print-disabled individuals and authorized entities can judicially enforce and seek legal confirmation of their rights to create and share accessible format copies. The remedies available to MT beneficiaries should include injunctions, damages, and other forms of relief necessary to fully vindicate these rights. National laws should also permit beneficiaries, authorized entities, and national human rights institutions to intervene in existing lawsuits.[71] States might also refer to the CRPD or other human rights instruments in MT-implementing

---

70. *Authors Guild, Inc. v. HathiTrust*, 755 F.3d 87, 92 (2d Cir. 2014).
71. From Exclusion to Equality: Realizing the Rights of Persons with Disabilities (Handbook for Parliamentarians on the Convention on the Rights of Persons with Disabilities and Its Optional Protocol) 103–04 (2007) [hereinafter Handbook for Parliamentarians].

legislation to assist courts and other institutions in interpreting the MT to realize its human rights objectives.[72]

Remedies also provide beneficiaries and authorized entities with the legal certainty and confidence to make, distribute, and share accessible format copies. Even when national law authorizes such activities, these actors may be inhibited from exercising their rights due to vague or ambiguous legal language or the activities of third parties.

States can minimize these chilling effects by ensuring that the exceptions to copyright in MT-implementing legislation are clearly drafted and communicate precisely and unambiguously the rights of beneficiaries and authorized entities to create and share accessible format copies. Such legislation should also avoid creating additional burdens—such as record-keeping standards, commercial availability requirements, or criteria for verifying beneficiary status—that may deter print-disabled persons and authorized entities from exercising their rights.

Although clearly defining rights and avoiding unnecessary burdens is an important first step, states should also adopt laws and policies that discourage copyright owners from invoking legal proceedings to impede print-disabled individuals and authorized entities from making and sharing accessible format copies. Abusive copyright litigation—and threats of such litigation—can significantly chill the exercise of MT rights. Under both IP law and human rights law, such lawsuits constitute an abuse of rights. States should consider creating civil remedies for harms associated with unfounded lawsuits (such as the common law tort of malicious prosecution), and procedural rules that authorize judges to shift the costs of litigation to the losing party (such as fee-shifting statutes).

States must also ensure that copyright owners do not use contracts to prevent beneficiaries and authorized entities from creating accessible format works, for example, by including clauses that restrict the use of electronic materials or prohibit circumvention of TPMs. Such contractual clauses defeat the object and purpose of the Treaty. States should therefore

---

72. Similarly, some countries provide that national disability law must be read in light of treaties protecting the rights of individuals with disabilities. *See* UNDP, OUR RIGHT TO KNOWLEDGE: LEGAL REVIEWS FOR THE RATIFICATION OF THE MARRAKESH TREATY FOR PERSONS WITH PRINT DISABILITIES IN ASIA AND THE PACIFIC 42 (2015).

consider including a provision in implementing legislation that renders void any contractual clauses that override MT-mandated exceptions and limitations.[73]

3.2. EMPOWER NATIONAL INSTITUTIONS

The Marrakesh Treaty gives states considerable discretion to select institutional arrangements to ensure the effective domestic implementation of the Treaty. States may, for example, vest authority over the Treaty in a national human rights institution (NHRI), an intellectual property office, or an agency charged with protecting civil liberties. They may also distribute these functions across several agencies or ministries.

3.2.1. *Human Rights Institutions*

One promising option is to connect implementation of the MT to the processes and institutions already established or envisioned for the CRPD and other human rights treaties. Linking implementation of the MT to these mechanisms helps to ensure that a country's efforts to comply with these treaties are consistent. It also enables the state to build on existing knowledge and expertise, avoid duplication of effort, coordinate activities among government agencies, and provide a coherent policy response to multiple international obligations.

More important, such a harmonized approach helps to ensure that domestic stakeholders—individuals with print disabilities, their advocacy organizations, and institutions charged with protecting human rights and combatting discrimination against persons with disabilities—participate in key decisions relating to how the MT is given effect. Whatever arrangement a state chooses, the responsible institutions must have the independence, powers, and resources to oversee all issues within their mandates, including, if applicable, the authority to investigate complaints about violations of MT access and sharing rights.

---

73. German law, for example, includes such a provision for any contract that overrides an exception to copyright. WIPO STUDY, *supra* note 4, at 45.

CRPD Article 33 requires states to vest authority over the CRPD in institutions outside of and within government—both an independent mechanism, such as a NHRI, as well as "focal" and "coordination" points within the government.

NHRIs, which are sometimes referred to as "human rights commissions" or "ombudsmen," typically share a number of common features. They are permanent institutions, usually created by legislation or executive decree. NHRIs are primarily administrative bodies that issue opinions and recommendations; many also have quasi-judicial powers to review complaints and resolve disputes relating to human rights issues. Principles governing the structure of NHRIs call for these institutions to have responsibility for, among other things, monitoring implementation of human rights treaties, reporting to international supervisory mechanisms about the extent of realization of rights, and promoting awareness of rights among the public.[74] The independence of NHRIs varies according to their relationship to the government, funding sources, membership, and manner of operation. Ideally, NHRIs should be fully independent of the government to enable them to more effectively promote, protect, and monitor implementation of human rights.

The CRPD also obligates states to create "focal" points within the government to protect the rights of disabled individuals. Some countries have established new agencies or offices, for example, within the ministry of justice. Others have augmented the powers of existing bodies, such as an agency charged with protecting civil liberties, and still others have distributed these functions across several agencies or ministries.[75] Focal points engage in a variety of tasks, such as suggesting revisions to national laws and policies, coordinating governmental activities and initiatives, raising awareness, encouraging participation of individuals with disabilities in policymaking, and collecting and analyzing data. Whatever arrangement a CRPD state party chooses, it must give the institution or institutions sufficient powers to oversee all government activities relating to the CRPD.[76] The focal point, for example, should have adequate resources

---

74. HANDBOOK FOR PARLIAMENTARIANS, *supra* note 71, at 98.
75. *See id.* at 94.
76. *Id.* at 94–95.

and permanent appointments and be established at the highest levels of government.[77]

The "coordination" point required by the CRPD is typically a public body that coordinates various state actions that affect individuals with disabilities.[78] It facilitates action relating to the CRPD across different areas and at different levels of government. A coordination point should be permanently established and facilitate the participation of individuals with disabilities in decision-making. Each state should ensure that the institutions and processes it charges with implementing and monitoring the MT are connected to this CRPD coordination point.

3.2.2. *Intellectual Property Institutions*

Inasmuch as the Marrakesh Treaty uses copyright tools to achieve human rights objectives, the domestic agencies and offices responsible for intellectual property laws and policies should also be involved in efforts to implement the Treaty. However, states should avoid vesting such offices or agencies with sole domestic authority over matters relating to the MT. The MT authorizes print-disabled individuals to access, create, and share accessible format copies without the authorization of rights holders. These objectives are in some tension with the mandates, working methods, cultures, and constituencies traditionally given to IP institutions.

Nonetheless, the expertise and relationships that these institutions have established over the years can be useful to achieving the MT's goals. For example, these offices understand the often technical aspects of IP law and policy. They also have the connections to private industry that can help to secure the support of rights holders for MT implementation.

Further, IP offices have assumed responsibility for enforcement efforts related to copyright exceptions in other contexts. The U.S. Library of Congress, for example, oversees the process of exempting actions from anti-circumvention legislation.[79] Because of the MT's dual nature

---

77. *Id.* at 94.
78. *Id.* at 96.
79. *See, e.g.,* Exemption to Prohibition on Circumvention of Copyright Protection Systems for Access Control Technologies, 37 C.F.R. § 201.40(b)(2) (2015).

as a human rights and an IP instrument, the most effective approach to implementation may therefore be to create shared authority between the domestic institutions in both areas.

3.2.3. Linking to the Marrakesh Treaty Assembly

Contracting Parties should link their national implementation mechanisms to the international institution created by the MT—the Assembly of Contracting Parties. According to Article 13(2), the Assembly is responsible for admitting intergovernmental organizations, deciding whether to convene a diplomatic conference to revise the MT, and, most relevant for present purposes, "deal[ing] with matters concerning the maintenance and development of this Treaty and the application and operation of this Treaty."

Each state is responsible for sending one delegate to the Assembly, who may be assisted by alternates, advisors, and experts. As part of creating national mechanisms to implement the MT, a state should identify an appropriate person to serve as its Assembly delegate and provide him or her with appropriate technical, legal, and other support. This delegate should ideally be someone with knowledge and experience in all three subject areas relevant to the Treaty—disability law, international human rights law, and IP law. An individual with expertise in IP law alone would not be well-suited to fulfill the MT's overriding human rights objectives. Further, states should give serious consideration to appointing one or more print-disabled individuals to serve as the delegate or as members of the delegation to the Assembly.

3.3. UNDERTAKE ENFORCEMENT ACTIVITIES

The domestic institutions that each Contracting Party creates and vests with authority over issues relating to the Marrakesh Treaty should engage in a variety of activities to ensure that print-disabled individuals benefit from the rights in the Treaty.

3.3.1. Monitor Rights

Providing beneficiaries and authorized entities with the ability to pursue remedies on their own behalf will not alone ensure effective enforcement of the Marrakesh Treaty. States must also affirmatively monitor the extent to which print-disabled persons are enjoying increased access to books and other covered works. Monitoring is essential to identify whether the rights conferred by the MT are being realized—that is, whether print-disabled individuals and authorized entities are in fact creating accessible format works and sharing them with beneficiaries in other countries.

By focusing on the actual enjoyment of rights, monitoring also generates crucial information that states can use to identify and tackle specific barriers to access. For example, monitoring may reveal that beneficiaries and their representative organizations are not taking advantage of their MT rights due to lack of knowledge, threats of litigation, the imposition of restrictive contracts, or efforts by third parties to limit access in other ways. Monitoring also helps to ensure that private actors do not create, due to their size or expertise, de facto monopolies that dominate the market for accessible format copies. In these and similar situations, a state will need to take additional affirmative steps to overcome these barriers to ensure that the Treaty's objectives are realized.

Monitoring requires an ongoing process of identifying barriers to access that should begin as soon as a state ratifies the MT and continue at periodic intervals after the Treaty is incorporated into domestic law. For example, the domestic institutions mentioned in the previous section should collect data about various aspects of compliance, such as the number of works in different accessible formats, the number of works imported and exported, and the number of users benefitting from access to covered works. Where possible, user data should be disaggregated by geographic region, gender, race, ethnicity or other minority status, income, and age, while respecting the privacy of beneficiary persons in accordance with Article 8. Disaggregated information can help to assess not only general levels of rights enjoyment in a particular country, but also whether access and sharing rights are enjoyed without discrimination, including by vulnerable, marginalized, and disadvantaged populations.

Monitoring processes should follow a national plan of action (discussed below) and be undertaken in consultation with beneficiaries and authorized entities. The domestic agencies and institutions responsible for monitoring should report regularly to the government, and the reports should be publicly available, including in accessible formats. Intellectual property offices, for example, might be tasked with reporting on the number and types of beneficiary persons enjoying MT rights and whether the number of accessible format copies has increased over time.

3.3.2. Enforce Legal Remedies

The domestic institution or institutions charged with responsibility for overseeing the MT should have the authority to pursue remedies on behalf of beneficiaries. Many states empower governmental bodies to seek direct enforcement of rights, both human rights and intellectual property rights. Such a body might monitor the exercise of, and investigate and remediate violations of, MT access and sharing rights, including, where appropriate, by bringing suit on behalf of persons whose rights have been violated.

The institution or institutions responsible for enforcing remedies might also encourage mediation with copyright owners if they engage in activities that impede the enjoyment of MT rights. NHRIs, for example, often have the authority to mediate or conciliate disputes.[80] Such dispute resolution processes could play an important role in reducing conflicts among copyright owners, beneficiaries, and authorized entities.

3.3.3. Create a National Plan of Action

States should consider integrating the Marrakesh Treaty's objectives into the national plans of action that they develop to implement their obligations under the CRPD and other human rights treaties.[81] A national action plan is typically a comprehensive document that contains both objectives and measurable outcomes set by the government in consultation with key

---

80. HANDBOOK FOR PARLIAMENTARIANS, *supra* note 71, at 98, 102–03.
81. Vienna Declaration and Programme of Action (25 June 1993), ¶ 71.

stakeholders. Efforts to implement the MT might be incorporated into existing national action plans to realize the rights of individuals with disabilities. The plans might, for example, increase awareness of Marrakesh Treaty rights, define objectives for expanding access to print materials in accessible formats, and collect data regarding such access. Australia's national plan of action, for example, calls for "[i]ncreased participation of people with disability, their families and carers in the social, cultural, religious, recreational and sporting life of the community."[82] Austria's national action plan emphasizes the importance of raising greater awareness of the issue of accessibility and tasks all government ministries with increased public relations work.[83]

A national action plan might also identify steps to increase access to accessible format copies. Albania's national plan, for example, calls for "[s]upport for the creation of 'talking books' and publications in brail [sic], that includes school curricula, technical, legal and artistic literature," and charges nongovernmental organizations and the Albanian Blind Association with this task.[84] National action plans also enable a state to identify with specificity which part of the government will be responsible for implementation of which objectives and to identify concrete steps for these entities to carry out. States should ensure that all aspects of the plan are accessible to individuals with print disabilities and their representative organizations.

States might also include in their national plans of action measures to encourage the development of technologies to enable print-disabled individuals to circumvent TPMs where needed to create accessible format copies. States should consider promoting such access-enhancing technologies through research and development policies. States should also consider eliminating legal liability for creating technologies used by beneficiaries and authorized entities to circumvent TPMs in order to exercise MT rights.[85]

---

82. Council of Australian Governments, National Disability Strategy 2010–2020, p. 31.
83. Austrian National Action Plan on Disability 2012–2020, pp. 43–44.
84. Republic of Albania, National Strategy on People with Disabilities, 2006, p. 33, http://www.osce.org/albania/40201?download=true.
85. Article 9(2)(h) of the CRPD requires ratifying states to "[p]romote the design, development, production and distribution of accessible information and communications technologies and systems at an early stage, so that these technologies and systems become accessible at minimum cost."

3.3.4. *Engage in Training and Outreach*

Training and outreach are critical for ensuring the effectiveness of a state's efforts to implement the Marrakesh Treaty. To achieve this goal, individuals with print disabilities, authorized entities, copyright owners, technology and software developers, and the public at large must understand that print-disabled individuals and authorized entities can make and share accessible format copies without permission of the copyright owner.

Training and outreach initiatives should target all of these actors. Outreach to copyright owners is especially important to reduce the risk that they may, for example, threaten individuals and authorized entities with unfounded litigation or impose contractual terms to defeat MT rights. Broader awareness-raising about the right to create and share accessible format copies will enable print-disabled persons and authorized entities to take advantage of the Treaty. Such knowledge will also help these actors to identify and overcome any burdens on the exercise of these rights and to pursue remedies for violations.

States should also widely publicize their ratification and implementation of the MT, including to schools, libraries, and national and local government agencies. Such dissemination may include, for example, public service announcements and "know your rights" letters. Disability rights organizations are crucial partners in efforts to reach individual beneficiaries; ideally, such organizations should be involved in every stage of implementing the MT, including an ongoing process of consultation. In addition, providing training and resources to government IP agencies would enable the staff of those agencies to respond to inquiries from copyright owners. Updates about implementing legislation could also be disseminated to lawyers via professional credentialing organizations, such as local or national bar organizations.

3.4. ENGAGE IN NATIONAL REPORTING

Marrakesh Treaty Contracting Parties should be prepared to provide information about the access and sharing rights of print-disabled individuals in periodic reports to the United Nations bodies that monitor state compliance with human rights. Three types of institutions engage in this kind of monitoring—the UN treaty bodies (including, in particular, the CRPD Committee), the UN Human Rights Council, and the UN special procedures.

3.4.1. UN Treaty Bodies

As noted in Chapter 1 of the Guide, each of the ten major UN human rights conventions, including the CRPD, creates an international monitoring mechanism known as a "treaty body"—a committee of experts charged with overseeing the implementation of that convention and assessing whether states are complying with the rights it protects. For the CRPD, these functions are performed by the CRPD Committee.

Treaty bodies engage in four primary activities—reviewing state reports, receiving communications, engaging in investigations, and publishing general comments. First, treaty bodies review reports, submitted by states parties every few years, that describe the measures they have adopted to give effect to the conventions. Committee members pose questions to the officials who present the reports and engage in a dialogue with the officials in public sessions in New York or Geneva. The treaty bodies end their review with concluding observations and recommendations for future action. For example, as mentioned in Section 1.1.4, when reviewing reports from CRPD states parties, the CRPD Committee has urged governments to ratify and implement the Marrakesh Treaty.

Second, the treaty bodies receive complaints, known as communications, from individuals who allege that a government has violated protected rights and freedoms. The committees review the communications, determine whether the state has breached the treaty, and recommend how the government should remedy the violation. However, the treaty bodies can review individual complaints only if the state has accepted an optional clause or optional protocol recognizing their authority to do so. As of October 2016, 92 of 168 member states of the CRPD had ratified the CRPD Optional Protocol.

Third, the CRPD Optional Protocol also authorizes the CRPD Committee to undertake inquiries in states parties if it receives reliable information indicating grave or systematic violations of the CRPD. As of the end of 2016, the Committee has not undertaken such an investigation.

Fourth, in addition to conclusions and recommendations on individual country reports, the treaty bodies publish "general comments" on issues and problems common to all states parties. For example, in 2014 the CRPD Committee published two general comments, one on accessibility for persons with disabilities and the other on equal recognition before the law. General comments describe protected rights and freedoms in ways that are often more detailed—and more relevant to contemporary circumstances—than the text of the human rights conventions themselves. With regard to the MT's access and sharing rights, the treaty bodies may provide normative guidance regarding human rights obligations that overlap with these provisions.

In sum, states may provide information to the CRPD Committee or to other treaty bodies in connection with periodic reporting, in response to communications by print-disabled individuals, or if the Committee initiates an inquiry into MT access and sharing rights. States that ratify the MT should provide such information to the CRPD Committee and, where relevant, to other treaty bodies to which they report, regarding their progress in implementing the MT and any barriers to implementation that they have encountered. To provide such information, national-level human rights and IP institutions charged with overseeing the MT will need to be involved in reporting to the treaty bodies. The officials who prepare a country's periodic reports or respond to communications or inquiries should solicit information from these institutions and other bodies charged with implementing and monitoring the MT.[86] States should be aware that print-disabled individuals and their representative organizations can also prepare and submit "shadow" reports to the Committee, which are designed to highlight gaps or inaccuracies in the government's official report.

---

86. Australia, for example, has established a detailed process for soliciting views of relevant government bodies in preparing its periodic reports. *See* Australian Human Rights Commission, Inquiry into the Commonwealth's Treaty-Making Process (Mar. 20, 2015), https://www.humanrights.gov.au/submissions/inquiry-commonwealth-s-treaty-making-process#fnB8.

None of the pronouncements of the treaty bodies—concluding observations on country reports, general comments, or decisions reviewing individual complaints—are legally binding. However, as official statements of the experts authorized to monitor compliance with international human rights law, the pronouncements have considerable persuasive and moral authority for states parties. For example, these documents have been cited favorably in litigation before international and national courts, have led some states to change national laws, and have been relied upon by civil society organizations to advocate for domestic legal and policy reforms.[87]

3.4.2. UN Charter Bodies

The UN Charter is the international convention that establishes the United Nations. Several institutions created under the authority of the UN Charter also exercise important functions relating to promoting and protecting human rights. The most important of these institutions is the Human Rights Council, an elected body of 47 UN member states. The Council's functions include the normative development of human rights standards, the appointment of independent experts to conduct studies and fact-finding missions to specific countries or on specific topics, consideration in public and private sessions of complaints alleging human rights violations, and the Universal Periodic Review (UPR) process, which assesses the human rights practices of all 193 UN member states once every four years. States that ratify the MT may be asked about their implementation of the Treaty as part of these processes.

Another human rights institution created under the UN Charter is the Office of the High Commissioner for Human Rights (OHCHR). Established in 1993, the OHCHR has a capacious mandate that includes promoting respect for human rights and deterring violations worldwide.

---

87. *See, e.g.*, Jarlath Clifford, *The UN Disability Convention and Its Impact on European Equality Law*, 6 EQUAL RTS. REV. 11 (2011); Rosanne van Alebeek & André Nollkaemper, *The Legal Status of Decisions by Human Rights Treaty Bodies in National Law*, in UN HUMAN RIGHTS TREATY BODIES: LAW AND LEGITIMACY 356 (Helen Keller & Geir Ulfstein eds., 2012).

3.4.3. UN Special Procedures

From time to time, the Human Rights Council appoints experts to address specific human rights topics or the human rights situation in particular countries. Collectively referred to as "special procedures," these appointees may be individuals ("Independent Experts" or "Special Rapporteurs") or groups ("Working Groups"). Experts serve in their individual capacities and engage in a variety of activities: collecting evidence and reporting on human rights violations, developing legal norms, communicating with governments about individual cases, and condemning violations. The reports and other documents generated by the special procedures are not legally binding, but they have significant moral authority and provide an important source of interpretive guidance for understanding the nature of human rights in particular areas. One expert whose work is directly relevant to the MT is the UN Special Rapporteur on the Rights of Persons with Disabilities.[88]

---

88. The position of the Special Rapporteur was first created in 1993 to monitor implementation of the UN Standard Rules for the Equalization of Opportunities of Persons with Disabilities.

Conclusion

The Marrakesh Treaty to Facilitate Access to Published Works for Persons Who Are Blind, Visually Impaired, or Otherwise Print Disabled is a watershed development in multiple respects. It is the first international legal instrument whose principal aim is to establish mandatory exceptions to the exclusive rights of copyright owners. It also marks the first time that the realization of international human rights has been the explicit objective of a World Intellectual Property Organization treaty and of the international system for the protection of intellectual property.

The Marrakesh Treaty requires ratifying countries to adopt legislation to enable individuals with print disabilities and authorized entities to make and share accessible format copies of covered copyrighted works. The Marrakesh Treaty also facilitates the cross-border exchange of such copies to expand their availability to print-disabled individuals around the world. The Treaty provides a range of options for states to meet these obligations, raising novel and often challenging questions of interpretation and implementation.

This Guide offers a comprehensive framework for government officials, policymakers, and disability rights organizations to interpret the Treaty and implement it in national law. The Guide's central premise is that the Marrakesh Treaty uses the institutions and doctrines of intellectual property law to achieve human rights objectives. This approach is grounded in the Treaty's Preamble, which references the Universal Declaration of Human Rights and the Convention on the Rights of Persons with Disabilities. The approach is also compatible with the international copyright system and furthers its overarching public welfare goals. Recognizing that states have obligations under both intellectual property and human rights treaties, the Guide offers general principles and specific policy recommendations to interpret and implement the Treaty consistently with both sets of commitments.

This Guide does not purport to answer all questions likely to arise as states implement and apply the Marrakesh Treaty in their national legal systems. States retain considerable discretion to choose how best to give effect to the Treaty. Many aspects of the Marrakesh Treaty will also evolve over time, shaped by the policy choices of government officials and civil society groups, by new technologies, and by the domestic and international institutions that monitor adherence to the Treaty. These developments should, however, always be guided by the practical needs of the print-disabled individuals who are the Treaty's principal beneficiaries. Keeping the welfare of these individuals in mind will not only strengthen the copyright and human rights regimes, it will also more fully realize the shared aspirations for human flourishing that the Treaty embodies.

APPENDIX 1

World Intellectual Property Organization, Extraordinary General Assembly: A Decision Text (December 18, 2012)

World Intellectual Property Organization

Geneva, December 18, 2012
PR/2012/727

This Assembly:

1. decides to convene a Diplomatic Conference on limitations and exceptions for visually impaired persons/persons with print disabilities to be held in June 2013. The mandate of this Conference is to negotiate and adopt a treaty on limitations and exceptions for visually impaired persons/persons with print disabilities (pursuant to the draft text in SCCR/25/2).
2. convenes a Preparatory Committee on December 18, 2012, to establish the necessary modalities of the Diplomatic Conference. The Preparatory Committee will consider at this time the draft Rules of Procedure to be presented for adoption to the Diplomatic Conference, the list of invitees to participate in the Conference, and the text of the draft letters of invitation, as well as any other document or organizational question relating to the Diplomatic Conference. The Preparatory Committee will also approve the Basic Proposal for the administrative and final provisions of the Treaty.
3. welcomes with gratitude the offer of the Kingdom of Morocco to host the Diplomatic Conference in June 2013.

APPENDIX 1

4. directs the SCCR to meet in special session for five days in February 2013 to expedite further text-based work on document SCCR/25/2, in order to reach a sufficient level of agreement on the text, and directs the Preparatory Committee to meet at the end of the February SCCR meeting to decide, if needed, whether additional work is required with the objective of holding a successful Conference in June 2013. It is understood that the Preparatory Committee will invite Observer Delegations and Observers.

5. agrees that document SCCR/25/2, the Draft Text of an International Agreement/Treaty on Limitations and Exceptions for Visually Impaired Persons/Persons with Print Disabilities, will constitute the substantive articles of the Basic Proposal for the Diplomatic Conference. The Preparatory Committee shall incorporate in the Basic Proposal such further agreements of the SCCR as are reached pursuant to paragraph (4) above, with the understanding that any Member State and the special delegation of the European Union may make proposals at the Diplomatic Conference.

APPENDIX 2

Marrakesh Treaty to Facilitate Access to Published Works for Persons Who Are Blind, Visually Impaired, or Otherwise Print Disabled (adopted on June 27, 2013, entered into force on September 30, 2016)

WIPO
WORLD INTELLECTUAL PROPERTY ORGANIZATION
VIP/DC/8
ORIGINAL:ENGLISH
DATE:JUNE 27, 2013

Diplomatic Conference to Conclude a Treaty to Facilitate Access to Published Works by Visually Impaired Persons and Persons with Print Disabilities

Marrakesh, June 17 to 28, 2013

adopted by the Diplomatic Conference

Preamble

The Contracting Parties,

Recalling the principles of non-discrimination, equal opportunity, accessibility and full and effective participation and inclusion in society, proclaimed in the Universal Declaration of Human Rights and the United Nations Convention on the Rights of Persons with Disabilities,

APPENDIX 2

Mindful of the challenges that are prejudicial to the complete development of persons with visual impairments or with other print disabilities, which limit their freedom of expression, including the freedom to seek, receive and impart information and ideas of all kinds on an equal basis with others, including through all forms of communication of their choice, their enjoyment of the right to education, and the opportunity to conduct research,

Emphasizing the importance of copyright protection as an incentive and reward for literary and artistic creations and of enhancing opportunities for everyone, including persons with visual impairments or with other print disabilities, to participate in the cultural life of the community, to enjoy the arts and to share scientific progress and its benefits,

Aware of the barriers of persons with visual impairments or with other print disabilities to access published works in achieving equal opportunities in society, and the need to both expand the number of works in accessible formats and to improve the circulation of such works,

Taking into account that the majority of persons with visual impairments or with other print disabilities live in developing and least-developed countries,

Recognizing that, despite the differences in national copyright laws, the positive impact of new information and communication technologies on the lives of persons with visual impairments or with other print disabilities may be reinforced by an enhanced legal framework at the international level,

Recognizing that many Member States have established limitations and exceptions in their national copyright laws for persons with visual impairments or with other print disabilities, yet there is a continuing shortage of available works in accessible format copies for such persons, and that considerable resources are required for their effort of making works accessible to these persons, and that the lack of possibilities of cross-border exchange of accessible format copies has necessitated duplication of these efforts,

Recognizing both the importance of rightholders' role in making their works accessible to persons with visual impairments or with other print disabilities and the importance of appropriate limitations and exceptions to make works accessible to these persons, particularly when the market is unable to provide such access,

Recognizing the need to maintain a balance between the effective protection of the rights of authors and the larger public interest, particularly education, research and access to information, and that such a balance must facilitate effective and timely access to works for the benefit of persons with visual impairments or with other print disabilities,

MARRAKESH TREATY

Reaffirming the obligations of Contracting Parties under the existing international treaties on the protection of copyright and the importance and flexibility of the three-step test for limitations and exceptions established in Article 9(2) of the Berne Convention for the Protection of Literary and Artistic Works and other international instruments,

Recalling the importance of the Development Agenda recommendations, adopted in 2007 by the General Assembly of the World Intellectual Property Organization (WIPO), which aim to ensure that development considerations form an integral part of the Organization's work,

Recognizing the importance of the international copyright system and desiring to harmonize limitations and exceptions with a view to facilitating access to and use of works by persons with visual impairments or with other print disabilities.

Have agreed as follows:

Article 1
Relation to other Conventions and Treaties

Nothing in this treaty shall derogate from any obligations that Contracting Parties have to each other under any other treaties, nor shall it prejudice any rights that a Contracting Party has under any other treaties.

Article 2
Definitions

For the purposes of this Treaty:

(a) "works" means literary and artistic works within the meaning of Article 2(1) of the Berne Convention for the Protection of Literary and Artistic Works, in the form of text, notation and/or related illustrations, whether published or otherwise made publicly available in any media[1];

(b) "accessible format copy" means a copy of a work in an alternative manner or form which gives a beneficiary person access to the work, including to permit the person to have access as feasibly and comfortably as a person without visual impairment or other print disability.

---

1. Agreed statement concerning Article 2(a): For the purposes of this Treaty, it is understood that this definition includes such works in audio form, such as audiobooks.

The accessible format copy is used exclusively by beneficiary persons and it must respect the integrity of the original work, taking due consideration of the changes needed to make the work accessible in the alternative format and of the accessibility needs of the beneficiary persons;

(c) "authorized entity" means an entity that is authorized or recognized by the government to provide education, instructional training, adaptive reading or information access to beneficiary persons on a non-profit basis. It also includes a government institution or non-profit organization that provides the same services to beneficiary persons as one of its primary activities or institutional obligations[2].

An authorized entity establishes and follows its own practices:

(i) to establish that the persons it serves are beneficiary persons;
(ii) to limit to beneficiary persons and/or authorized entities its distribution and making available of accessible format copies;
(iii) to discourage the reproduction, distribution and making available of unauthorized copies; and
(iv) to maintain due care in, and records of, its handling of copies of works, while respecting the privacy of beneficiary persons in accordance with Article 8.

Article 3
Beneficiary Persons

A beneficiary person is a person who:

(a) is blind;
(b) has a visual impairment or a perceptual or reading disability which cannot be improved to give visual function substantially equivalent to that of a person who has no such impairment or disability and so is unable to read printed works to substantially the same degree as a person without an impairment or disability; or[3]

---

2. Agreed statement concerning Article 2(c): For the purposes of this Treaty, it is understood that "entities recognized by the government" may include entities receiving financial support from the government to provide education, instructional training, adaptive reading or information access to beneficiary persons on a non-profit basis.
3. Agreed statement concerning Article 3(b): Nothing in this language implies that "cannot be improved" requires the use of all possible medical diagnostic procedures and treatments.

(c) is otherwise unable, through physical disability, to hold or manipulate a book or to focus or move the eyes to the extent that would be normally acceptable for reading;

regardless of any other disabilities.

Article 4
National Law Limitations and Exceptions Regarding Accessible Format Copies

1. (a) Contracting Parties shall provide in their national copyright laws for a limitation or exception to the right of reproduction, the right of distribution, and the right of making available to the public as provided by the WIPO Copyright Treaty (WCT), to facilitate the availability of works in accessible format copies for beneficiary persons. The limitation or exception provided in national law should permit changes needed to make the work accessible in the alternative format.
   (b) Contracting Parties may also provide a limitation or exception to the right of public performance to facilitate access to works for beneficiary persons.
2. A Contracting Party may fulfill Article 4(1) for all rights identified therein by providing a limitation or exception in its national copyright law such that:
   (a) Authorized entities shall be permitted, without the authorization of the copyright rightholder, to make an accessible format copy of a work, obtain from another authorized entity an accessible format copy, and supply those copies to beneficiary persons by any means, including by non-commercial lending or by electronic communication by wire or wireless means, and undertake any intermediate steps to achieve those objectives, when all of the following conditions are met:
      (i) the authorized entity wishing to undertake said activity has lawful access to that work or a copy of that work;
      (ii) the work is converted to an accessible format copy, which may include any means needed to navigate information in the accessible format, but does not introduce changes other than those needed to make the work accessible to the beneficiary person;
      (iii) such accessible format copies are supplied exclusively to be used by beneficiary persons; and
      (iv) the activity is undertaken on a non-profit basis;

and
  (b) A beneficiary person, or someone acting on his or her behalf including a primary caretaker or caregiver, may make an accessible format copy of a work for the personal use of the beneficiary person or otherwise may assist the beneficiary person to make and use accessible format copies where the beneficiary person has lawful access to that work or a copy of that work.
3. A Contracting Party may fulfill Article 4(1) by providing other limitations or exceptions in its national copyright law pursuant to Articles 10 and 11[4].
4. A Contracting Party may confine limitations or exceptions under this Article to works which, in the particular accessible format, cannot be obtained commercially under reasonable terms for beneficiary persons in that market. Any Contracting Party availing itself of this possibility shall so declare in a notification deposited with the Director General of WIPO at the time of ratification of, acceptance of or accession to this Treaty or at any time thereafter[5].
5. It shall be a matter for national law to determine whether limitations or exceptions under this Article are subject to remuneration.

Article 5
Cross-Border Exchange of Accessible Format Copies

1. Contracting Parties shall provide that if an accessible format copy is made under a limitation or exception or pursuant to operation of law, that accessible format copy may be distributed or made available by an authorized entity to a beneficiary person or an authorized entity in another Contracting Party[6].
2. A Contracting Party may fulfill Article 5(1) by providing a limitation or exception in its national copyright law such that:
   (a) authorized entities shall be permitted, without the authorization of the rightholder, to distribute or make available for the exclusive

---

4. Agreed Statement concerning Article 4(3): It is understood that this paragraph neither reduces nor extends the scope of applicability of limitations and exceptions permitted under the Berne Convention, as regards the right of translation, with respect to persons with visual impairments or with other print disabilities.
5. Agreed Statement concerning Article 4(4): It is understood that a commercial availability requirement does not prejudge whether or not a limitation or exception under this Article is consistent with the three-step test.
6. Agreed statement concerning Article 5(1): It is further understood that nothing in this Treaty reduces or extends the scope of exclusive rights under any other treaty.

use of beneficiary persons accessible format copies to an authorized entity in another Contracting Party; and

(b) authorized entities shall be permitted, without the authorization of the rightholder and pursuant to Article 2(c), to distribute or make available accessible format copies to a beneficiary person in another Contracting Party;

provided that prior to the distribution or making available the originating authorized entity did not know or have reasonable grounds to know that the accessible format copy would be used for other than beneficiary persons.[7]

3. A Contracting Party may fulfill Article 5(1) by providing other limitations or exceptions in its national copyright law pursuant to Articles 5(4), 10 and 11.

4. (a) When an authorized entity in a Contracting Party receives accessible format copies pursuant to Article 5(1) and that Contracting Party does not have obligations under Article 9 of the Berne Convention, it will ensure, consistent with its own legal system and practices, that the accessible format copies are only reproduced, distributed or made available for the benefit of beneficiary persons in that Contracting Party's jurisdiction.

(b) The distribution and making available of accessible format copies by an authorized entity pursuant to Article 5(1) shall be limited to that jurisdiction unless the Contracting Party is a Party to the WIPO Copyright Treaty or otherwise limits limitations and exceptions implementing this Treaty to the right of distribution and the right of making available to the public to certain special cases which do not conflict with a normal exploitation of the work and do not unreasonably prejudice the legitimate interests of the rightholder.[8,9]

---

7. Agreed statement concerning Article 5(2): It is understood that, to distribute or make available accessible format copies directly to a beneficiary person in another Contracting Party, it may be appropriate for an authorized entity to apply further measures to confirm that the person it is serving is a beneficiary person and to follow its own practices as described in Article 2.
8. Agreed statement concerning Article 5(4)(b): It is understood that nothing in this Treaty requires or implies that a Contracting Party adopt or apply the three-step test beyond its obligations under this instrument or under other international treaties.
9. Agreed statement concerning Article 5(4)(b): It is understood that nothing in this Treaty creates any obligations for a Contracting Party to ratify or accede to the WCT or to comply with any of its provisions and nothing in this Treaty prejudices any rights, limitations and exceptions contained in the WCT.

(c) Nothing in this Article affects the determination of what constitutes an act of distribution or an act of making available to the public.
5. Nothing in this Treaty shall be used to address the issue of exhaustion of rights.

Article 6
Importation of Accessible Format Copies

To the extent that the national law of a Contracting Party would permit a beneficiary person, someone acting on his or her behalf, or an authorized entity, to make an accessible format copy of a work, the national law of that Contracting Party shall also permit them to import an accessible format copy for the benefit of beneficiary persons, without the authorization of the rightholder.[10]

Article 7
Obligations Concerning Technological Measures

Contracting Parties shall take appropriate measures, as necessary, to ensure that when they provide adequate legal protection and effective legal remedies against the circumvention of effective technological measures, this legal protection does not prevent beneficiary persons from enjoying the limitations and exceptions provided for in this Treaty.[11]

Article 8
Respect for Privacy

In the implementation of the limitations and exceptions provided for in this Treaty, Contracting Parties shall endeavor to protect the privacy of beneficiary persons on an equal basis with others.

---

10. Agreed statement concerning Article 6: It is understood that the Contracting Parties have the same flexibilities set out in Article 4 when implementing their obligations under Article 6.
11. Agreed statement concerning Article 7: It is understood that authorized entities, in various circumstances, choose to apply technological measures in the making, distribution and making available of accessible format copies and nothing herein disturbs such practices when in accordance with national law.

Article 9
Cooperation to Facilitate Cross-Border Exchange

1. Contracting Parties shall endeavor to foster the cross-border exchange of accessible format copies by encouraging the voluntary sharing of information to assist authorized entities in identifying one another. The International Bureau of WIPO shall establish an information access point for this purpose.
2. Contracting Parties undertake to assist their authorized entities engaged in activities under Article 5 to make information available regarding their practices pursuant to Article 2(c), both through the sharing of information among authorized entities, and through making available information on their policies and practices, including related to cross-border exchange of accessible format copies, to interested parties and members of the public as appropriate.
3. The International Bureau of WIPO is invited to share information, where available, about the functioning of this Treaty.
4. Contracting Parties recognize the importance of international cooperation and its promotion, in support of national efforts for realization of the purpose and objectives of this Treaty.[12]

Article 10
General Principles on Implementation

1. Contracting Parties undertake to adopt the measures necessary to ensure the application of this Treaty.
2. Nothing shall prevent Contracting Parties from determining the appropriate method of implementing the provisions of this Treaty within their own legal system and practice.[13]
3. Contracting Parties may fulfill their rights and obligations under this Treaty through limitations or exceptions specifically for the benefit of beneficiary persons, other limitations or exceptions, or a combination thereof, within their national legal system and practice. These may include judicial,

---

12. Agreed statement concerning Article 9: It is understood that Article 9 does not imply mandatory registration for authorized entities nor does it constitute a precondition for authorized entities to engage in activities recognized under this Treaty; but it provides for a possibility for sharing information to facilitate the cross-border exchange of accessible format copies.
13. Agreed Statement concerning Article 10(2): It is understood that when a work qualifies as a work under Article 2, including such works in audio form, the limitations and exceptions provided for by this Treaty apply *mutatis mutandis* to related rights as necessary to make the accessible format copy, to distribute it and to make it available to beneficiary persons.

administrative or regulatory determinations for the benefit of beneficiary persons as to fair practices, dealings or uses to meet their needs consistent with the Contracting Parties' rights and obligations under the Berne Convention, other international treaties, and Article 11.

Article 11
General Obligations on Limitations and Exceptions

In adopting measures necessary to ensure the application of this Treaty, a Contracting Party may exercise the rights and shall comply with the obligations that that Contracting Party has under the Berne Convention, the Agreement on Trade-Related Aspects of Intellectual Property Rights and the WIPO Copyright Treaty, including their interpretative agreements so that:

(a) in accordance with Article 9(2) of the Berne Convention, a Contracting Party may permit the reproduction of works in certain special cases provided that such reproduction does not conflict with a normal exploitation of the work and does not unreasonably prejudice the legitimate interests of the author;

(b) in accordance with Article 13 of the Agreement on Trade-Related Aspects of Intellectual Property Rights, a Contracting Party shall confine limitations or exceptions to exclusive rights to certain special cases which do not conflict with a normal exploitation of the work and do not unreasonably prejudice the legitimate interests of the rightholder;

(c) in accordance with Article 10(1) of the WIPO Copyright Treaty, a Contracting Party may provide for limitations of or exceptions to the rights granted to authors under the WCT in certain special cases, that do not conflict with a normal exploitation of the work and do not unreasonably prejudice the legitimate interests of the author;

(d) in accordance with Article 10(2) of the WIPO Copyright Treaty, a Contracting Party shall confine, when applying the Berne Convention, any limitations of or exceptions to rights to certain special cases that do not conflict with a normal exploitation of the work and do not unreasonably prejudice the legitimate interests of the author.

Article 12
Other Limitations and Exceptions

1. Contracting Parties recognize that a Contracting Party may implement in its national law other copyright limitations and exceptions for the

benefit of beneficiary persons than are provided by this Treaty having regard to that Contracting Party's economic situation, and its social and cultural needs, in conformity with that Contracting Party's international rights and obligations, and in the case of a least-developed country taking into account its special needs and its particular international rights and obligations and flexibilities thereof.
2. This Treaty is without prejudice to other limitations and exceptions for persons with disabilities provided by national law.

Article 13
Assembly

1. (a) The Contracting Parties shall have an Assembly.
   (b) Each Contracting Party shall be represented in the Assembly by one delegate who may be assisted by alternate delegates, advisors and experts.
   (c) The expenses of each delegation shall be borne by the Contracting Party that has appointed the delegation. The Assembly may ask WIPO to grant financial assistance to facilitate the participation of delegations of Contracting Parties that are regarded as developing countries in conformity with the established practice of the General Assembly of the United Nations or that are countries in transition to a market economy.
2. (a) The Assembly shall deal with matters concerning the maintenance and development of this Treaty and the application and operation of this Treaty.
   (b) The Assembly shall perform the function allocated to it under Article 15 in respect of the admission of certain intergovernmental organizations to become party to this Treaty.
   (c) The Assembly shall decide the convocation of any diplomatic conference for the revision of this Treaty and give the necessary instructions to the Director General of WIPO for the preparation of such diplomatic conference.
3. (a) Each Contracting Party that is a State shall have one vote and shall vote only in its own name.
   (b) Any Contracting Party that is an intergovernmental organization may participate in the vote, in place of its Member States, with a number of votes equal to the number of its Member States which are party to this Treaty. No such intergovernmental organization

shall participate in the vote if any one of its Member States exercises its right to vote and vice versa.
4. The Assembly shall meet upon convocation by the Director General and, in the absence of exceptional circumstances, during the same period and at the same place as the General Assembly of WIPO.
5. The Assembly shall endeavor to take its decisions by consensus and shall establish its own rules of procedure, including the convocation of extraordinary sessions, the requirements of a quorum and, subject to the provisions of this Treaty, the required majority for various kinds of decisions.

Article 14
International Bureau

The International Bureau of WIPO shall perform the administrative tasks concerning this Treaty.

Article 15
Eligibility for Becoming Party to the Treaty

(1) Any Member State of WIPO may become party to this Treaty.
(2) The Assembly may decide to admit any intergovernmental organization to become party to this Treaty which declares that it is competent in respect of, and has its own legislation binding on all its Member States on, matters covered by this Treaty and that it has been duly authorized, in accordance with its internal procedures, to become party to this Treaty.
(3) The European Union, having made the declaration referred to in the preceding paragraph at the Diplomatic Conference that has adopted this Treaty, may become party to this Treaty.

Article 16
Rights and Obligations under the Treaty

Subject to any specific provisions to the contrary in this Treaty, each Contracting Party shall enjoy all of the rights and assume all of the obligations under this Treaty.

Article 17
Signature of the Treaty

This Treaty shall be open for signature at the Diplomatic Conference in Marrakesh, and thereafter at the headquarters of WIPO by any eligible party for one year after its adoption.

Article 18
Entry into Force of the Treaty

This Treaty shall enter into force three months after 20 eligible parties referred to in Article 15 have deposited their instruments of ratification or accession.

Article 19
Effective Date of Becoming Party to the Treaty

This Treaty shall bind:

(a) the 20 eligible parties referred to in Article 18, from the date on which this Treaty has entered into force;
(b) each other eligible party referred to in Article 15, from the expiration of three months from the date on which it has deposited its instrument of ratification or accession with the Director General of WIPO.

Article 20
Denunciation of the Treaty

This Treaty may be denounced by any Contracting Party by notification addressed to the Director General of WIPO. Any denunciation shall take effect one year from the date on which the Director General of WIPO received the notification.

Article 21
Languages of the Treaty

(1) This Treaty is signed in a single original in English, Arabic, Chinese, French, Russian and Spanish languages, the versions in all these languages being equally authentic.

(2) An official text in any language other than those referred to in Article 21(1) shall be established by the Director General of WIPO on the request of an interested party, after consultation with all the interested parties. For the purposes of this paragraph, "interested party" means any Member State of WIPO whose official language, or one of whose official languages, is involved and the European Union, and any other intergovernmental organization that may become party to this Treaty, if one of its official languages is involved.

Article 22
Depositary

The Director General of WIPO is the depositary of this Treaty.

Done in Marrakesh on the 27th day of June, 2013

APPENDIX 3

Signatories and Contracting Parties to the Marrakesh Treaty (as of October 31, 2016)

Contracting Party	Signature	Instrument	In Force
Afghanistan	June 28, 2013		
Argentina	May 21, 2014	Ratification: April 1, 2015	September 30, 2016
Australia	June 23, 2014	Ratification: December 10, 2015	September 30, 2016
Austria	June 25, 2014		
Belgium	June 25, 2014		
Bosnia and Herzegovina	June 28, 2013		
Botswana		Accession: October 5, 2016	January 5, 2017

(*Continued*)

APPENDIX 3

Contracting Party	Signature	Instrument	In Force
Brazil	June 28, 2013	Ratification: December 11, 2015	September 30, 2016
Burkina Faso	June 28, 2013		
Burundi	June 28, 2013		
Cambodia	June 28, 2013		
Cameroon	June 28, 2013		
Canada		Accession: June 30, 2016	September 30, 2016
Central African Republic	June 28, 2013		
Chad	June 28, 2013		
Chile	June 28, 2013	Ratification: May 10, 2016	September 30, 2016
China	June 28, 2013		
Colombia	June 28, 2013		
Comoros	June 28, 2013		
Congo	June 28, 2013		
Costa Rica	June 28, 2013		
Côte d'Ivoire	June 28, 2013		
Cyprus	June 28, 2013		
Czech Republic	June 24, 2014		
Democratic People's Republic of Korea	June 28, 2013	Ratification: February 19, 2016	September 30, 2016
Denmark	June 28, 2013		
Djibouti	June 28, 2013		
Dominican Republic	June 28, 2013		

MARRAKESH TREATY-SIGNATORIES & CONTRACTING PARTIES

Contracting Party	Signature	Instrument	In Force
Ecuador	May 8, 2014	Ratification: June 29, 2016	September 30, 2016
El Salvador	October 11, 2013	Ratification: October 1, 2014	September 30, 2016
Ethiopia	June 28, 2013		
European Union (EU)	April 30, 2014		
Finland	June 20, 2014		
France	April 30, 2014		
Germany	June 20, 2014		
Ghana	June 28, 2013		
Greece	April 30, 2014		
Guatemala	June 2, 2014	Ratification: June 29, 2016	September 30, 2016
Guinea	June 28, 2013		
Haiti	June 28, 2013		
Holy See	June 28, 2013		
India	April 30, 2014	Ratification: June 24, 2014	September 30, 2016
Indonesia	September 24, 2013		
Iran (Islamic Republic of)	June 27, 2014		
Ireland	June 20, 2014		
Israel		Accession: March 21, 2016	September 30, 2016
Jordan	June 28, 2013		

(*Continued*)

APPENDIX 3

Contracting Party	Signature	Instrument	In Force
Kenya	June 28, 2013		
Lebanon	June 28, 2013		
Liberia		Accession: October 6, 2016	January 6, 2017
Lithuania	September 27, 2013		
Luxembourg	June 28, 2013		
Mali	June 28, 2013	Ratification: December 16, 2014	September 30, 2016
Mauritania	June 28, 2013		
Mauritius	June 28, 2013		
Mexico	June 25, 2014	Ratification: July 29, 2015	September 30, 2016
Mongolia	June 28, 2013	Ratification: September 23, 2015	September 30, 2016
Morocco	June 28, 2013		
Mozambique	August 22, 2013		
Namibia	August 12, 2013		
Nepal	June 28, 2013		
Nigeria	June 28, 2013		
Norway	June 20, 2014		
Panama	June 28, 2013		
Paraguay	June 28, 2013	Ratification: January 20, 2015	September 30, 2016
Peru	June 28, 2013	Ratification: February 2, 2016	September 30, 2016
Poland	June 24, 2014		

MARRAKESH TREATY-SIGNATORIES & CONTRACTING PARTIES

Contracting Party	Signature	Instrument	In Force
Republic of Korea	June 26, 2014	Ratification: October 8, 2015	September 30, 2016
Republic of Moldova	June 28, 2013		
Saint Vincent and the Grenadines		Accession: September 5, 2016	December 5, 2016
Sao Tome and Principe	June 28, 2013		
Senegal	June 28, 2013		
Sierra Leone	June 28, 2013		
Singapore		Accession: March 30, 2015	September 30, 2016
Slovenia	May 16, 2014		
Sri Lanka		Accession: October 5, 2016	January 5, 2017
Sudan	June 28, 2013		
Switzerland	June 28, 2013		
Syrian Arab Republic	November 22, 2013		
Togo	June 28, 2013		
Tunisia	June 28, 2013	Ratification: September 7, 2016	December 7, 2016
Turkey	November 1, 2013		
Uganda	June 28, 2013		
United Arab Emirates		Accession: October 15, 2014	September 30, 2016
United Kingdom	June 28, 2013		

(*Continued*)

APPENDIX 3

Contracting Party	Signature	Instrument	In Force
United States of America	October 2, 2013		
Uruguay	June 28, 2013	Ratification: December 1, 2014	September 30, 2016
Zimbabwe	October 2, 2013		

APPENDIX 4

Convention on the Rights of Persons with Disabilities (adopted on December 13, 2006, entered into force on May 3, 2008)

Preamble

The States Parties to the present Convention,

(a) *Recalling* the principles proclaimed in the Charter of the United Nations which recognize the inherent dignity and worth and the equal and inalienable rights of all members of the human family as the foundation of freedom, justice and peace in the world,
(b) *Recognizing* that the United Nations, in the Universal Declaration of Human Rights and in the International Covenants on Human Rights, has proclaimed and agreed that everyone is entitled to all the rights and freedoms set forth therein, without distinction of any kind,
(c) *Reaffirming* the universality, indivisibility, interdependence and inter-relatedness of all human rights and fundamental freedoms and the need for persons with disabilities to be guaranteed their full enjoyment without discrimination,
(d) *Recalling* the International Covenant on Economic, Social and Cultural Rights, the International Covenant on Civil and Political Rights, the International Convention on the Elimination of All

Forms of Racial Discrimination, the Convention on the Elimination of All Forms of Discrimination against Women, the Convention against Torture and Other Cruel, Inhuman or Degrading Treatment or Punishment, the Convention on the Rights of the Child, and the International Convention on the Protection of the Rights of All Migrant Workers and Members of Their Families,

(e) *Recognizing* that disability is an evolving concept and that disability results from the interaction between persons with impairments and attitudinal and environmental barriers that hinders their full and effective participation in society on an equal basis with others,

(f) *Recognizing* the importance of the principles and policy guidelines contained in the World Programme of Action concerning Disabled Persons and in the Standard Rules on the Equalization of Opportunities for Persons with Disabilities in influencing the promotion, formulation and evaluation of the policies, plans, programmes and actions at the national, regional and international levels to further equalize opportunities for persons with disabilities,

(g) *Emphasizing* the importance of mainstreaming disability issues as an integral part of relevant strategies of sustainable development,

(h) *Recognizing also* that discrimination against any person on the basis of disability is a violation of the inherent dignity and worth of the human person,

(i) *Recognizing further* the diversity of persons with disabilities,

(j) *Recognizing* the need to promote and protect the human rights of all persons with disabilities, including those who require more intensive support,

(k) *Concerned* that, despite these various instruments and undertakings, persons with disabilities continue to face barriers in their participation as equal members of society and violations of their human rights in all parts of the world,

(l) *Recognizing* the importance of international cooperation for improving the living conditions of persons with disabilities in every country, particularly in developing countries,

(m) *Recognizing* the valued existing and potential contributions made by persons with disabilities to the overall well-being and diversity of their communities, and that the promotion of the full enjoyment by persons with disabilities of their human rights and fundamental freedoms and of full participation by persons with disabilities will result in their enhanced sense of belonging and in significant advances in the human, social and economic development of society and the eradication of poverty,

(n) *Recognizing* the importance for persons with disabilities of their individual autonomy and independence, including the freedom to make their own choices,

(o) *Considering* that persons with disabilities should have the opportunity to be actively involved in decision-making processes about policies and programmes, including those directly concerning them,

(p) *Concerned* about the difficult conditions faced by persons with disabilities who are subject to multiple or aggravated forms of discrimination on the basis of race, colour, sex, language, religion, political or other opinion, national, ethnic, indigenous or social origin, property, birth, age or other status,

(q) *Recognizing* that women and girls with disabilities are often at greater risk, both within and outside the home of violence, injury or abuse, neglect or negligent treatment, maltreatment or exploitation,

(r) *Recognizing* that children with disabilities should have full enjoyment of all human rights and fundamental freedoms on an equal basis with other children, and recalling obligations to that end undertaken by States Parties to the Convention on the Rights of the Child,

(s) *Emphasizing* the need to incorporate a gender perspective in all efforts to promote the full enjoyment of human rights and fundamental freedoms by persons with disabilities,

(t) *Highlighting* the fact that the majority of persons with disabilities live in conditions of poverty, and in this regard recognizing the critical need to address the negative impact of poverty on persons with disabilities,

(u) *Bearing in mind* that conditions of peace and security based on full respect for the purposes and principles contained in the Charter of the United Nations and observance of applicable human rights instruments are indispensable for the full protection of persons with disabilities, in particular during armed conflicts and foreign occupation,

(v) *Recognizing* the importance of accessibility to the physical, social, economic and cultural environment, to health and education and to information and communication, in enabling persons with disabilities to fully enjoy all human rights and fundamental freedoms,

(w) *Realizing* that the individual, having duties to other individuals and to the community to which he or she belongs, is under a responsibility to strive for the promotion and observance of the rights recognized in the International Bill of Human Rights,

(x) *Convinced* that the family is the natural and fundamental group unit of society and is entitled to protection by society and the State, and that persons with disabilities and their family members should receive the necessary protection and assistance to enable families to contribute towards the full and equal enjoyment of the rights of persons with disabilities,

(y) *Convinced* that a comprehensive and integral international convention to promote and protect the rights and dignity of persons with disabilities will make a significant contribution to redressing the profound social disadvantage of persons with disabilities and promote their participation in the civil, political, economic, social and cultural spheres with equal opportunities, in both developing and developed countries,

Have agreed as follows:

Article 1
Purpose

The purpose of the present Convention is to promote, protect and ensure the full and equal enjoyment of all human rights and fundamental freedoms by all persons with disabilities, and to promote respect for their inherent dignity.

Persons with disabilities include those who have long-term physical, mental, intellectual or sensory impairments which in interaction with various barriers may hinder their full and effective participation in society on an equal basis with others.

Article 2
Definitions

For the purposes of the present Convention:

- "Communication" includes languages, display of text, Braille, tactile communication, large print, accessible multimedia as well as written, audio, plain-language, human-reader and augmentative and alternative modes, means and formats of communication, including accessible information and communication technology;
- "Language" includes spoken and signed languages and other forms of non-spoken languages;
- "Discrimination on the basis of disability" means any distinction, exclusion or restriction on the basis of disability which has the purpose or effect of impairing or nullifying the recognition, enjoyment or exercise, on an equal basis with others, of all human rights and fundamental freedoms in the political, economic, social, cultural, civil or any other field. It includes all forms of discrimination, including denial of reasonable accommodation;
- "Reasonable accommodation" means necessary and appropriate modification and adjustments not imposing a disproportionate or undue burden, where needed in a particular case, to ensure to persons with disabilities the enjoyment or exercise on an equal basis with others of all human rights and fundamental freedoms;

"Universal design" means the design of products, environments, programmes and services to be usable by all people, to the greatest extent possible, without the need for adaptation or specialized design. "Universal design" shall not exclude assistive devices for particular groups of persons with disabilities where this is needed.

Article 3
General principles

The principles of the present Convention shall be:

(a) Respect for inherent dignity, individual autonomy including the freedom to make one's own choices, and independence of persons;
(b) Non-discrimination;
(c) Full and effective participation and inclusion in society;
(d) Respect for difference and acceptance of persons with disabilities as part of human diversity and humanity;
(e) Equality of opportunity;
(f) Accessibility;
(g) Equality between men and women;
(h) Respect for the evolving capacities of children with disabilities and respect for the right of children with disabilities to preserve their identities.

Article 4
General obligations

1. States Parties undertake to ensure and promote the full realization of all human rights and fundamental freedoms for all persons with disabilities without discrimination of any kind on the basis of disability. To this end, States Parties undertake:
    (a) To adopt all appropriate legislative, administrative and other measures for the implementation of the rights recognized in the present Convention;
    (b) To take all appropriate measures, including legislation, to modify or abolish existing laws, regulations, customs and practices that constitute discrimination against persons with disabilities;
    (c) To take into account the protection and promotion of the human rights of persons with disabilities in all policies and programmes;
    (d) To refrain from engaging in any act or practice that is inconsistent with the present Convention and to ensure that public authorities and institutions act in conformity with the present Convention;

(e) To take all appropriate measures to eliminate discrimination on the basis of disability by any person, organization or private enterprise;

(f) To undertake or promote research and development of universally designed goods, services, equipment and facilities, as defined in article 2 of the present Convention, which should require the minimum possible adaptation and the least cost to meet the specific needs of a person with disabilities, to promote their availability and use, and to promote universal design in the development of standards and guidelines;

(g) To undertake or promote research and development of, and to promote the availability and use of new technologies, including information and communications technologies, mobility aids, devices and assistive technologies, suitable for persons with disabilities, giving priority to technologies at an affordable cost;

(h) To provide accessible information to persons with disabilities about mobility aids, devices and assistive technologies, including new technologies, as well as other forms of assistance, support services and facilities;

(i) To promote the training of professionals and staff working with persons with disabilities in the rights recognized in this Convention so as to better provide the assistance and services guaranteed by those rights.

2. With regard to economic, social and cultural rights, each State Party undertakes to take measures to the maximum of its available resources and, where needed, within the framework of international cooperation, with a view to achieving progressively the full realization of these rights, without prejudice to those obligations contained in the present Convention that are immediately applicable according to international law.

3. In the development and implementation of legislation and policies to implement the present Convention, and in other decision-making processes concerning issues relating to persons with disabilities, States Parties shall closely consult with and actively involve persons with disabilities, including children with disabilities, through their representative organizations.

4. Nothing in the present Convention shall affect any provisions which are more conducive to the realization of the rights of persons with disabilities and which may be contained in the law of a State Party or international law in force for that State. There shall be no restriction upon or derogation from any of the human rights and fundamental freedoms recognized or existing in any State Party to the present Convention pursuant to law, conventions, regulation or custom on the pretext that the present Convention does not recognize such rights or freedoms or that it recognizes them to a lesser extent.

5. The provisions of the present Convention shall extend to all parts of federal states without any limitations or exceptions.

Article 5
Equality and non-discrimination

1. States Parties recognize that all persons are equal before and under the law and are entitled without any discrimination to the equal protection and equal benefit of the law.
2. States Parties shall prohibit all discrimination on the basis of disability and guarantee to persons with disabilities equal and effective legal protection against discrimination on all grounds.
3. In order to promote equality and eliminate discrimination, States Parties shall take all appropriate steps to ensure that reasonable accommodation is provided.
4. Specific measures which are necessary to accelerate or achieve de facto equality of persons with disabilities shall not be considered discrimination under the terms of the present Convention.

Article 6
Women with disabilities

1. States Parties recognize that women and girls with disabilities are subject to multiple discrimination, and in this regard shall take measures to ensure the full and equal enjoyment by them of all human rights and fundamental freedoms.
2. States Parties shall take all appropriate measures to ensure the full development, advancement and empowerment of women, for the purpose of guaranteeing them the exercise and enjoyment of the human rights and fundamental freedoms set out in the present Convention.

Article 7
Children with disabilities

1. States Parties shall take all necessary measures to ensure the full enjoyment by children with disabilities of all human rights and fundamental freedoms on an equal basis with other children.
2. In all actions concerning children with disabilities, the best interests of the child shall be a primary consideration.
3. States Parties shall ensure that children with disabilities have the right to express their views freely on all matters affecting them, their views

being given due weight in accordance with their age and maturity, on an equal basis with other children, and to be provided with disability and age-appropriate assistance to realize that right.

Article 8
Awareness-raising

1. States Parties undertake to adopt immediate, effective and appropriate measures:
    (a) To raise awareness throughout society, including at the family level, regarding persons with disabilities, and to foster respect for the rights and dignity of persons with disabilities;
    (b) To combat stereotypes, prejudices and harmful practices relating to persons with disabilities, including those based on sex and age, in all areas of life;
    (c) To promote awareness of the capabilities and contributions of persons with disabilities.
2. Measures to this end include:
    (a) Initiating and maintaining effective public awareness campaigns designed:
        (i) To nurture receptiveness to the rights of persons with disabilities;
        (ii) To promote positive perceptions and greater social awareness towards persons with disabilities;
        (iii) To promote recognition of the skills, merits and abilities of persons with disabilities, and of their contributions to the workplace and the labour market;
    (b) Fostering at all levels of the education system, including in all children from an early age, an attitude of respect for the rights of persons with disabilities;
    (c) Encouraging all organs of the media to portray persons with disabilities in a manner consistent with the purpose of the present Convention;
    (d) Promoting awareness-training programmes regarding persons with disabilities and the rights of persons with disabilities.

Article 9
Accessibility

1. To enable persons with disabilities to live independently and participate fully in all aspects of life, States Parties shall take appropriate measures

to ensure to persons with disabilities access, on an equal basis with others, to the physical environment, to transportation, to information and communications, including information and communications technologies and systems, and to other facilities and services open or provided to the public, both in urban and in rural areas. These measures, which shall include the identification and elimination of obstacles and barriers to accessibility, shall apply to, inter alia:
- (a) Buildings, roads, transportation and other indoor and outdoor facilities, including schools, housing, medical facilities and workplaces;
- (b) Information, communications and other services, including electronic services and emergency services.

2. States Parties shall also take appropriate measures to:
   - (a) Develop, promulgate and monitor the implementation of minimum standards and guidelines for the accessibility of facilities and services open or provided to the public;
   - (b) Ensure that private entities that offer facilities and services which are open or provided to the public take into account all aspects of accessibility for persons with disabilities;
   - (c) Provide training for stakeholders on accessibility issues facing persons with disabilities;
   - (d) Provide in buildings and other facilities open to the public signage in Braille and in easy to read and understand forms;
   - (e) Provide forms of live assistance and intermediaries, including guides, readers and professional sign language interpreters, to facilitate accessibility to buildings and other facilities open to the public;
   - (f) Promote other appropriate forms of assistance and support to persons with disabilities to ensure their access to information;
   - (g) Promote access for persons with disabilities to new information and communications technologies and systems, including the Internet;
   - (h) Promote the design, development, production and distribution of accessible information and communications technologies and systems at an early stage, so that these technologies and systems become accessible at minimum cost.

Article 10
Right to life

States Parties reaffirm that every human being has the inherent right to life and shall take all necessary measures to ensure its effective enjoyment by persons with disabilities on an equal basis with others.

Article 11
Situations of risk and humanitarian emergencies

States Parties shall take, in accordance with their obligations under international law, including international humanitarian law and international human rights law, all necessary measures to ensure the protection and safety of persons with disabilities in situations of risk, including situations of armed conflict, humanitarian emergencies and the occurrence of natural disasters.

Article 12
Equal recognition before the law

1. States Parties reaffirm that persons with disabilities have the right to recognition everywhere as persons before the law.
2. States Parties shall recognize that persons with disabilities enjoy legal capacity on an equal basis with others in all aspects of life.
3. States Parties shall take appropriate measures to provide access by persons with disabilities to the support they may require in exercising their legal capacity.
4. States Parties shall ensure that all measures that relate to the exercise of legal capacity provide for appropriate and effective safeguards to prevent abuse in accordance with international human rights law. Such safeguards shall ensure that measures relating to the exercise of legal capacity respect the rights, will and preferences of the person, are free of conflict of interest and undue influence, are proportional and tailored to the person's circumstances, apply for the shortest time possible and are subject to regular review by a competent, independent and impartial authority or judicial body. The safeguards shall be proportional to the degree to which such measures affect the person's rights and interests.
5. Subject to the provisions of this article, States Parties shall take all appropriate and effective measures to ensure the equal right of persons with disabilities to own or inherit property, to control their own financial affairs and to have equal access to bank loans, mortgages and other forms of financial credit, and shall ensure that persons with disabilities are not arbitrarily deprived of their property.

Article 13
Access to justice

1. States Parties shall ensure effective access to justice for persons with disabilities on an equal basis with others, including through the provision of procedural and age-appropriate accommodations, in order to

facilitate their effective role as direct and indirect participants, including as witnesses, in all legal proceedings, including at investigative and other preliminary stages.
2. In order to help to ensure effective access to justice for persons with disabilities, States Parties shall promote appropriate training for those working in the field of administration of justice, including police and prison staff.

Article 14
Liberty and security of the person

1. States Parties shall ensure that persons with disabilities, on an equal basis with others:
   (a) Enjoy the right to liberty and security of person;
   (b) Are not deprived of their liberty unlawfully or arbitrarily, and that any deprivation of liberty is in conformity with the law, and that the existence of a disability shall in no case justify a deprivation of liberty.
2. States Parties shall ensure that if persons with disabilities are deprived of their liberty through any process, they are, on an equal basis with others, entitled to guarantees in accordance with international human rights law and shall be treated in compliance with the objectives and principles of this Convention, including by provision of reasonable accommodation.

Article 15
Freedom from torture or cruel, inhuman or degrading treatment or punishment

1. No one shall be subjected to torture or to cruel, inhuman or degrading treatment or punishment. In particular, no one shall be subjected without his or her free consent to medical or scientific experimentation.
2. States Parties shall take all effective legislative, administrative, judicial or other measures to prevent persons with disabilities, on an equal basis with others, from being subjected to torture or cruel, inhuman or degrading treatment or punishment.

Article 16
Freedom from exploitation, violence and abuse

1. States Parties shall take all appropriate legislative, administrative, social, educational and other measures to protect persons with disabilities,

both within and outside the home, from all forms of exploitation, violence and abuse, including their gender-based aspects.
2. States Parties shall also take all appropriate measures to prevent all forms of exploitation, violence and abuse by ensuring, inter alia, appropriate forms of gender- and age-sensitive assistance and support for persons with disabilities and their families and caregivers, including through the provision of information and education on how to avoid, recognize and report instances of exploitation, violence and abuse. States Parties shall ensure that protection services are age-, gender- and disability-sensitive.
3. In order to prevent the occurrence of all forms of exploitation, violence and abuse, States Parties shall ensure that all facilities and programmes designed to serve persons with disabilities are effectively monitored by independent authorities.
4. States Parties shall take all appropriate measures to promote the physical, cognitive and psychological recovery, rehabilitation and social reintegration of persons with disabilities who become victims of any form of exploitation, violence or abuse, including through the provision of protection services. Such recovery and reintegration shall take place in an environment that fosters the health, welfare, self-respect, dignity and autonomy of the person and takes into account gender- and age-specific needs.
5. States Parties shall put in place effective legislation and policies, including women- and child-focused legislation and policies, to ensure that instances of exploitation, violence and abuse against persons with disabilities are identified, investigated and, where appropriate, prosecuted.

Article 17
Protecting the integrity of the person

Every person with disabilities has a right to respect for his or her physical and mental integrity on an equal basis with others.

Article 18
Liberty of movement and nationality

1. States Parties shall recognize the rights of persons with disabilities to liberty of movement, to freedom to choose their residence and to a nationality, on an equal basis with others, including by ensuring that persons with disabilities:
    (a) Have the right to acquire and change a nationality and are not deprived of their nationality arbitrarily or on the basis of disability;

(b) Are not deprived, on the basis of disability, of their ability to obtain, possess and utilize documentation of their nationality or other documentation of identification, or to utilize relevant processes such as immigration proceedings, that may be needed to facilitate exercise of the right to liberty of movement;
(c) Are free to leave any country, including their own;
(d) Are not deprived, arbitrarily or on the basis of disability, of the right to enter their own country.
2. Children with disabilities shall be registered immediately after birth and shall have the right from birth to a name, the right to acquire a nationality and, as far as possible, the right to know and be cared for by their parents.

Article 19
Living independently and being included in the community

States Parties to this Convention recognize the equal right of all persons with disabilities to live in the community, with choices equal to others, and shall take effective and appropriate measures to facilitate full enjoyment by persons with disabilities of this right and their full inclusion and participation in the community, including by ensuring that:

(a) Persons with disabilities have the opportunity to choose their place of residence and where and with whom they live on an equal basis with others and are not obliged to live in a particular living arrangement;
(b) Persons with disabilities have access to a range of in-home, residential and other community support services, including personal assistance necessary to support living and inclusion in the community, and to prevent isolation or segregation from the community;
(c) Community services and facilities for the general population are available on an equal basis to persons with disabilities and are responsive to their needs.

Article 20
Personal mobility

States Parties shall take effective measures to ensure personal mobility with the greatest possible independence for persons with disabilities, including by:

(a) Facilitating the personal mobility of persons with disabilities in the manner and at the time of their choice, and at affordable cost;

(b) Facilitating access by persons with disabilities to quality mobility aids, devices, assistive technologies and forms of live assistance and intermediaries, including by making them available at affordable cost;
(c) Providing training in mobility skills to persons with disabilities and to specialist staff working with persons with disabilities;
(d) Encouraging entities that produce mobility aids, devices and assistive technologies to take into account all aspects of mobility for persons with disabilities.

Article 21
Freedom of expression and opinion, and access to information

States Parties shall take all appropriate measures to ensure that persons with disabilities can exercise the right to freedom of expression and opinion, including the freedom to seek, receive and impart information and ideas on an equal basis with others and through all forms of communication of their choice, as defined in article 2 of the present Convention, including by:

(a) Providing information intended for the general public to persons with disabilities in accessible formats and technologies appropriate to different kinds of disabilities in a timely manner and without additional cost;
(b) Accepting and facilitating the use of sign languages, Braille, augmentative and alternative communication, and all other accessible means, modes and formats of communication of their choice by persons with disabilities in official interactions;
(c) Urging private entities that provide services to the general public, including through the Internet, to provide information and services in accessible and usable formats for persons with disabilities;
(d) Encouraging the mass media, including providers of information through the Internet, to make their services accessible to persons with disabilities;
(e) Recognizing and promoting the use of sign languages.

Article 22
Respect for privacy

1. No person with disabilities, regardless of place of residence or living arrangements, shall be subjected to arbitrary or unlawful interference with his or her privacy, family, home or correspondence or other types of communication or to unlawful attacks on his or her honour and reputation. Persons with disabilities have the right to the protection of the law against such interference or attacks.

2. States Parties shall protect the privacy of personal, health and rehabilitation information of persons with disabilities on an equal basis with others.

Article 23
Respect for home and the family

1. States Parties shall take effective and appropriate measures to eliminate discrimination against persons with disabilities in all matters relating to marriage, family, parenthood and relationships, on an equal basis with others, so as to ensure that:
   (a) The right of all persons with disabilities who are of marriageable age to marry and to found a family on the basis of free and full consent of the intending spouses is recognized;
   (b) The rights of persons with disabilities to decide freely and responsibly on the number and spacing of their children and to have access to age-appropriate information, reproductive and family planning education are recognized, and the means necessary to enable them to exercise these rights are provided;
   (c) Persons with disabilities, including children, retain their fertility on an equal basis with others.
2. States Parties shall ensure the rights and responsibilities of persons with disabilities, with regard to guardianship, wardship, trusteeship, adoption of children or similar institutions, where these concepts exist in national legislation; in all cases the best interests of the child shall be paramount. States Parties shall render appropriate assistance to persons with disabilities in the performance of their child-rearing responsibilities.
3. States Parties shall ensure that children with disabilities have equal rights with respect to family life. With a view to realizing these rights, and to prevent concealment, abandonment, neglect and segregation of children with disabilities, States Parties shall undertake to provide early and comprehensive information, services and support to children with disabilities and their families.
4. States Parties shall ensure that a child shall not be separated from his or her parents against their will, except when competent authorities subject to judicial review determine, in accordance with applicable law and procedures, that such separation is necessary for the best interests of the child. In no case shall a child be separated from parents on the basis of a disability of either the child or one or both of the parents.
5. States Parties shall, where the immediate family is unable to care for a child with disabilities, undertake every effort to provide alternative care within the wider family, and failing that, within the community in a family setting.

Article 24
Education

1. States Parties recognize the right of persons with disabilities to education. With a view to realizing this right without discrimination and on the basis of equal opportunity, States Parties shall ensure an inclusive education system at all levels and life long learning directed to:
    (a) The full development of human potential and sense of dignity and self-worth, and the strengthening of respect for human rights, fundamental freedoms and human diversity;
    (b) The development by persons with disabilities of their personality, talents and creativity, as well as their mental and physical abilities, to their fullest potential;
    (c) Enabling persons with disabilities to participate effectively in a free society.
2. In realizing this right, States Parties shall ensure that:
    (a) Persons with disabilities are not excluded from the general education system on the basis of disability, and that children with disabilities are not excluded from free and compulsory primary education, or from secondary education, on the basis of disability;
    (b) Persons with disabilities can access an inclusive, quality and free primary education and secondary education on an equal basis with others in the communities in which they live;
    (c) Reasonable accommodation of the individual's requirements is provided;
    (d) Persons with disabilities receive the support required, within the general education system, to facilitate their effective education;
    (e) Effective individualized support measures are provided in environments that maximize academic and social development, consistent with the goal of full inclusion.
3. States Parties shall enable persons with disabilities to learn life and social development skills to facilitate their full and equal participation in education and as members of the community. To this end, States Parties shall take appropriate measures, including:
    (a) Facilitating the learning of Braille, alternative script, augmentative and alternative modes, means and formats of communication and orientation and mobility skills, and facilitating peer support and mentoring;
    (b) Facilitating the learning of sign language and the promotion of the linguistic identity of the deaf community;
    (c) Ensuring that the education of persons, and in particular children, who are blind, deaf or deafblind, is delivered in the most appropriate languages and modes and means of communication for the

individual, and in environments which maximize academic and social development.

4. In order to help ensure the realization of this right, States Parties shall take appropriate measures to employ teachers, including teachers with disabilities, who are qualified in sign language and/or Braille, and to train professionals and staff who work at all levels of education. Such training shall incorporate disability awareness and the use of appropriate augmentative and alternative modes, means and formats of communication, educational techniques and materials to support persons with disabilities.

5. States Parties shall ensure that persons with disabilities are able to access general tertiary education, vocational training, adult education and lifelong learning without discrimination and on an equal basis with others. To this end, States Parties shall ensure that reasonable accommodation is provided to persons with disabilities.

Article 25
Health

States Parties recognize that persons with disabilities have the right to the enjoyment of the highest attainable standard of health without discrimination on the basis of disability. States Parties shall take all appropriate measures to ensure access for persons with disabilities to health services that are gender-sensitive, including health-related rehabilitation. In particular, States Parties shall:

(a) Provide persons with disabilities with the same range, quality and standard of free or affordable health care and programmes as provided to other persons, including in the area of sexual and reproductive health and population-based public health programmes;

(b) Provide those health services needed by persons with disabilities specifically because of their disabilities, including early identification and intervention as appropriate, and services designed to minimize and prevent further disabilities, including among children and older persons;

(c) Provide these health services as close as possible to people's own communities, including in rural areas;

(d) Require health professionals to provide care of the same quality to persons with disabilities as to others, including on the basis of free and informed consent by, inter alia, raising awareness of the human rights, dignity, autonomy and needs of persons with disabilities through training and the promulgation of ethical standards for public and private health care;

(e) Prohibit discrimination against persons with disabilities in the provision of health insurance, and life insurance where such insurance is

permitted by national law, which shall be provided in a fair and reasonable manner;
(f) Prevent discriminatory denial of health care or health services or food and fluids on the basis of disability.

Article 26
Habilitation and rehabilitation

1. States Parties shall take effective and appropriate measures, including through peer support, to enable persons with disabilities to attain and maintain maximum independence, full physical, mental, social and vocational ability, and full inclusion and participation in all aspects of life. To that end, States Parties shall organize, strengthen and extend comprehensive habilitation and rehabilitation services and programmes, particularly in the areas of health, employment, education and social services, in such a way that these services and programmes:
   (a) Begin at the earliest possible stage, and are based on the multidisciplinary assessment of individual needs and strengths;
   (b) Support participation and inclusion in the community and all aspects of society, are voluntary, and are available to persons with disabilities as close as possible to their own communities, including in rural areas.
2. States Parties shall promote the development of initial and continuing training for professionals and staff working in habilitation and rehabilitation services.
3. States Parties shall promote the availability, knowledge and use of assistive devices and technologies, designed for persons with disabilities, as they relate to habilitation and rehabilitation.

Article 27
Work and employment

1. States Parties recognize the right of persons with disabilities to work, on an equal basis with others; this includes the right to the opportunity to gain a living by work freely chosen or accepted in a labour market and work environment that is open, inclusive and accessible to persons with disabilities. States Parties shall safeguard and promote the realization of the right to work, including for those who acquire a disability during the course of employment, by taking appropriate steps, including through legislation, to, inter alia:
   (a) Prohibit discrimination on the basis of disability with regard to all matters concerning all forms of employment, including conditions

of recruitment, hiring and employment, continuance of employment, career advancement and safe and healthy working conditions;
(b) Protect the rights of persons with disabilities, on an equal basis with others, to just and favourable conditions of work, including equal opportunities and equal remuneration for work of equal value, safe and healthy working conditions, including protection from harassment, and the redress of grievances;
(c) Ensure that persons with disabilities are able to exercise their labour and trade union rights on an equal basis with others;
(d) Enable persons with disabilities to have effective access to general technical and vocational guidance programmes, placement services and vocational and continuing training;
(e) Promote employment opportunities and career advancement for persons with disabilities in the labour market, as well as assistance in finding, obtaining, maintaining and returning to employment;
(f) Promote opportunities for self-employment, entrepreneurship, the development of cooperatives and starting one's own business;
(g) Employ persons with disabilities in the public sector;
(h) Promote the employment of persons with disabilities in the private sector through appropriate policies and measures, which may include affirmative action programmes, incentives and other measures;
(i) Ensure that reasonable accommodation is provided to persons with disabilities in the workplace;
(j) Promote the acquisition by persons with disabilities of work experience in the open labour market;
(k) Promote vocational and professional rehabilitation, job retention and return-to-work programmes for persons with disabilities.
2. States Parties shall ensure that persons with disabilities are not held in slavery or in servitude, and are protected, on an equal basis with others, from forced or compulsory labour.

Article 28
Adequate standard of living and social protection

1. States Parties recognize the right of persons with disabilities to an adequate standard of living for themselves and their families, including adequate food, clothing and housing, and to the continuous improvement of living conditions, and shall take appropriate steps to safeguard and promote the realization of this right without discrimination on the basis of disability.
2. States Parties recognize the right of persons with disabilities to social protection and to the enjoyment of that right without discrimination on

the basis of disability, and shall take appropriate steps to safeguard and promote the realization of this right, including measures:

(a) To ensure equal access by persons with disabilities to clean water services, and to ensure access to appropriate and affordable services, devices and other assistance for disability-related needs;

(b) To ensure access by persons with disabilities, in particular women and girls with disabilities and older persons with disabilities, to social protection programmes and poverty reduction programmes;

(c) To ensure access by persons with disabilities and their families living in situations of poverty to assistance from the State with disability-related expenses, including adequate training, counselling, financial assistance and respite care;

(d) To ensure access by persons with disabilities to public housing programmes;

(e) To ensure equal access by persons with disabilities to retirement benefits and programmes.

Article 29
Participation in political and public life

States Parties shall guarantee to persons with disabilities political rights and the opportunity to enjoy them on an equal basis with others, and shall undertake to:

(a) Ensure that persons with disabilities can effectively and fully participate in political and public life on an equal basis with others, directly or through freely chosen representatives, including the right and opportunity for persons with disabilities to vote and be elected, inter alia, by:

  (i) Ensuring that voting procedures, facilities and materials are appropriate, accessible and easy to understand and use;

  (ii) Protecting the right of persons with disabilities to vote by secret ballot in elections and public referendums without intimidation, and to stand for elections, to effectively hold office and perform all public functions at all levels of government, facilitating the use of assistive and new technologies where appropriate;

  (iii) Guaranteeing the free expression of the will of persons with disabilities as electors and to this end, where necessary, at their request, allowing assistance in voting by a person of their own choice;

(b) Promote actively an environment in which persons with disabilities can effectively and fully participate in the conduct of public affairs,

without discrimination and on an equal basis with others, and encourage their participation in public affairs, including:
  (i) Participation in non-governmental organizations and associations concerned with the public and political life of the country, and in the activities and administration of political parties;
  (ii) Forming and joining organizations of persons with disabilities to represent persons with disabilities at international, national, regional and local levels.

Article 30
Participation in cultural life, recreation, leisure and sport

1. States Parties recognize the right of persons with disabilities to take part on an equal basis with others in cultural life, and shall take all appropriate measures to ensure that persons with disabilities:
   (a) Enjoy access to cultural materials in accessible formats;
   (b) Enjoy access to television programmes, films, theatre and other cultural activities, in accessible formats;
   (c) Enjoy access to places for cultural performances or services, such as theatres, museums, cinemas, libraries and tourism services, and, as far as possible, enjoy access to monuments and sites of national cultural importance.
2. States Parties shall take appropriate measures to enable persons with disabilities to have the opportunity to develop and utilize their creative, artistic and intellectual potential, not only for their own benefit, but also for the enrichment of society.
3. States Parties shall take all appropriate steps, in accordance with international law, to ensure that laws protecting intellectual property rights do not constitute an unreasonable or discriminatory barrier to access by persons with disabilities to cultural materials.
4. Persons with disabilities shall be entitled, on an equal basis with others, to recognition and support of their specific cultural and linguistic identity, including sign languages and deaf culture.
5. With a view to enabling persons with disabilities to participate on an equal basis with others in recreational, leisure and sporting activities, States Parties shall take appropriate measures:
   (a) To encourage and promote the participation, to the fullest extent possible, of persons with disabilities in mainstream sporting activities at all levels;
   (b) To ensure that persons with disabilities have an opportunity to organize, develop and participate in disability-specific sporting

and recreational activities and, to this end, encourage the provision, on an equal basis with others, of appropriate instruction, training and resources;
(c) To ensure that persons with disabilities have access to sporting, recreational and tourism venues;
(d) To ensure that children with disabilities have equal access with other children to participation in play, recreation and leisure and sporting activities, including those activities in the school system;
(e) To ensure that persons with disabilities have access to services from those involved in the organization of recreational, tourism, leisure and sporting activities.

Article 31
Statistics and data collection

1. States Parties undertake to collect appropriate information, including statistical and research data, to enable them to formulate and implement policies to give effect to the present Convention. The process of collecting and maintaining this information shall:
   (a) Comply with legally established safeguards, including legislation on data protection, to ensure confidentiality and respect for the privacy of persons with disabilities;
   (b) Comply with internationally accepted norms to protect human rights and fundamental freedoms and ethical principles in the collection and use of statistics.
2. The information collected in accordance with this article shall be disaggregated, as appropriate, and used to help assess the implementation of States Parties' obligations under the present Convention and to identify and address the barriers faced by persons with disabilities in exercising their rights.
3. States Parties shall assume responsibility for the dissemination of these statistics and ensure their accessibility to persons with disabilities and others.

Article 32
International cooperation

1. States Parties recognize the importance of international cooperation and its promotion, in support of national efforts for the realization of

the purpose and objectives of the present Convention, and will undertake appropriate and effective measures in this regard, between and among States and, as appropriate, in partnership with relevant international and regional organizations and civil society, in particular organizations of persons with disabilities. Such measures could include, inter alia:
  (a) Ensuring that international cooperation, including international development programmes, is inclusive of and accessible to persons with disabilities;
  (b) Facilitating and supporting capacity-building, including through the exchange and sharing of information, experiences, training programmes and best practices;
  (c) Facilitating cooperation in research and access to scientific and technical knowledge;
  (d) Providing, as appropriate, technical and economic assistance, including by facilitating access to and sharing of accessible and assistive technologies, and through the transfer of technologies.
2. The provisions of this article are without prejudice to the obligations of each State Party to fulfil its obligations under the present Convention.

Article 33
National implementation and monitoring

1. States Parties, in accordance with their system of organization, shall designate one or more focal points within government for matters relating to the implementation of the present Convention, and shall give due consideration to the establishment or designation of a coordination mechanism within government to facilitate related action in different sectors and at different levels.
2. States Parties shall, in accordance with their legal and administrative systems, maintain, strengthen, designate or establish within the State Party, a framework, including one or more independent mechanisms, as appropriate, to promote, protect and monitor implementation of the present Convention. When designating or establishing such a mechanism, States Parties shall take into account the principles relating to the status and functioning of national institutions for protection and promotion of human rights.
3. Civil society, in particular persons with disabilities and their representative organizations, shall be involved and participate fully in the monitoring process.

Article 34
Committee on the Rights of Persons with Disabilities

1. There shall be established a Committee on the Rights of Persons with Disabilities (hereafter referred to as "the Committee"), which shall carry out the functions hereinafter provided.
2. The Committee shall consist, at the time of entry into force of the present Convention, of twelve experts. After an additional sixty ratifications or accessions to the Convention, the membership of the Committee shall increase by six members, attaining a maximum number of eighteen members.
3. The members of the Committee shall serve in their personal capacity and shall be of high moral standing and recognized competence and experience in the field covered by the present Convention. When nominating their candidates, States Parties are invited to give due consideration to the provision set out in article 4, paragraph 3 of the present Convention.
4. The members of the Committee shall be elected by States Parties, consideration being given to equitable geographical distribution, representation of the different forms of civilization and of the principal legal systems, balanced gender representation and participation of experts with disabilities.
5. The members of the Committee shall be elected by secret ballot from a list of persons nominated by the States Parties from among their nationals at meetings of the Conference of States Parties. At those meetings, for which two thirds of States Parties shall constitute a quorum, the persons elected to the Committee shall be those who obtain the largest number of votes and an absolute majority of the votes of the representatives of States Parties present and voting.
6. The initial election shall be held no later than six months after the date of entry into force of the present Convention. At least four months before the date of each election, the Secretary-General of the United Nations shall address a letter to the States Parties inviting them to submit the nominations within two months. The Secretary-General shall subsequently prepare a list in alphabetical order of all persons thus nominated, indicating the State Parties which have nominated them, and shall submit it to the States Parties to the present Convention.
7. The members of the Committee shall be elected for a term of four years. They shall be eligible for re-election once. However, the term of six of the members elected at the first election shall expire at the end of two years; immediately after the first election, the names of these six members shall be chosen by lot by the chairperson of the meeting referred to in paragraph 5 of this article.

8. The election of the six additional members of the Committee shall be held on the occasion of regular elections, in accordance with the relevant provisions of this article.
9. If a member of the Committee dies or resigns or declares that for any other cause she or he can no longer perform her or his duties, the State Party which nominated the member shall appoint another expert possessing the qualifications and meeting the requirements set out in the relevant provisions of this article, to serve for the remainder of the term.
10. The Committee shall establish its own rules of procedure.
11. The Secretary-General of the United Nations shall provide the necessary staff and facilities for the effective performance of the functions of the Committee under the present Convention, and shall convene its initial meeting.
12. With the approval of the General Assembly, the members of the Committee established under the present Convention shall receive emoluments from United Nations resources on such terms and conditions as the Assembly may decide, having regard to the importance of the Committee's responsibilities.
13. The members of the Committee shall be entitled to the facilities, privileges and immunities of experts on mission for the United Nations as laid down in the relevant sections of the Convention on the Privileges and Immunities of the United Nations.

Article 35
Reports by States Parties

1. Each State Party shall submit to the Committee, through the Secretary-General of the United Nations, a comprehensive report on measures taken to give effect to its obligations under the present Convention and on the progress made in that regard, within two years after the entry into force of the present Convention for the State Party concerned.
2. Thereafter, States Parties shall submit subsequent reports at least every four years and further whenever the Committee so requests.
3. The Committee shall decide any guidelines applicable to the content of the reports.
4. A State Party which has submitted a comprehensive initial report to the Committee need not, in its subsequent reports, repeat information previously provided. When preparing reports to the Committee, States Parties are invited to consider doing so in an open and transparent

process and to give due consideration to the provision set out in article 4, paragraph 3 of the present Convention.
5. Reports may indicate factors and difficulties affecting the degree of fulfilment of obligations under the present Convention.

Article 36
Consideration of reports

1. Each report shall be considered by the Committee, which shall make such suggestions and general recommendations on the report as it may consider appropriate and shall forward these to the State Party concerned. The State Party may respond with any information it chooses to the Committee. The Committee may request further information from States Parties relevant to the implementation of the present Convention.
2. If a State Party is significantly overdue in the submission of a report, the Committee may notify the State Party concerned of the need to examine the implementation of the present Convention in that State Party, on the basis of reliable information available to the Committee, if the relevant report is not submitted within three months following the notification. The Committee shall invite the State Party concerned to participate in such examination. Should the State Party respond by submitting the relevant report, the provisions of paragraph 1 of this article will apply.
3. The Secretary-General of the United Nations shall make available the reports to all States Parties.
4. States Parties shall make their reports widely available to the public in their own countries and facilitate access to the suggestions and general recommendations relating to these reports.
5. The Committee shall transmit, as it may consider appropriate, to the specialized agencies, funds and programmes of the United Nations, and other competent bodies, reports from States Parties in order to address a request or indication of a need for technical advice or assistance contained therein, along with the Committee's observations and recommendations, if any, on these requests or indications.

Article 37
Cooperation between States Parties and the Committee

1. Each State Party shall cooperate with the Committee and assist its members in the fulfilment of their mandate.
2. In its relationship with States Parties, the Committee shall give due consideration to ways and means of enhancing national capacities for the

implementation of the present Convention, including through international cooperation.

Article 38
Relationship of the Committee with other bodies

In order to foster the effective implementation of the present Convention and to encourage international cooperation in the field covered by the present Convention:

(a) The specialized agencies and other United Nations organs shall be entitled to be represented at the consideration of the implementation of such provisions of the present Convention as fall within the scope of their mandate. The Committee may invite the specialized agencies and other competent bodies as it may consider appropriate to provide expert advice on the implementation of the Convention in areas falling within the scope of their respective mandates. The Committee may invite specialized agencies and other United Nations organs to submit reports on the implementation of the Convention in areas falling within the scope of their activities;

(b) The Committee, as it discharges its mandate, shall consult, as appropriate, other relevant bodies instituted by international human rights treaties, with a view to ensuring the consistency of their respective reporting guidelines, suggestions and general recommendations, and avoiding duplication and overlap in the performance of their functions.

Article 39
Report of the Committee

The Committee shall report every two years to the General Assembly and to the Economic and Social Council on its activities, and may make suggestions and general recommendations based on the examination of reports and information received from the States Parties. Such suggestions and general recommendations shall be included in the report of the Committee together with comments, if any, from States Parties.

Article 40
Conference of States Parties

1. The States Parties shall meet regularly in a Conference of States Parties in order to consider any matter with regard to the implementation of the present Convention.

2. No later than six months after the entry into force of the present Convention, the Conference of the States Parties shall be convened by the Secretary-General of the United Nations. The subsequent meetings shall be convened by the Secretary-General of the United Nations biennially or upon the decision of the Conference of States Parties.

Article 41
Depositary

The Secretary-General of the United Nations shall be the depositary of the present Convention.

Article 42
Signature

The present Convention shall be open for signature by all States and by regional integration organizations at United Nations Headquarters in New York as of 30 March 2007.

Article 43
Consent to be bound

The present Convention shall be subject to ratification by signatory States and to formal confirmation by signatory regional integration organizations. It shall be open for accession by any State or regional integration organization which has not signed the Convention.

Article 44
Regional integration organizations

1. "Regional integration organization" shall mean an organization constituted by sovereign States of a given region, to which its member States have transferred competence in respect of matters governed by this Convention. Such organizations shall declare, in their instruments of formal confirmation or accession, the extent of their competence with respect to matters governed by this Convention. Subsequently, they shall inform the depositary of any substantial modification in the extent of their competence.

2. References to "States Parties" in the present Convention shall apply to such organizations within the limits of their competence.
3. For the purposes of article 45, paragraph 1, and article 47, paragraphs 2 and 3, any instrument deposited by a regional integration organization shall not be counted.
4. Regional integration organizations, in matters within their competence, may exercise their right to vote in the Conference of States Parties, with a number of votes equal to the number of their member States that are Parties to this Convention. Such an organization shall not exercise its right to vote if any of its member States exercises its right, and vice versa.

Article 45
Entry into force

1. The present Convention shall enter into force on the thirtieth day after the deposit of the twentieth instrument of ratification or accession.
2. For each State or regional integration organization ratifying, formally confirming or acceding to the Convention after the deposit of the twentieth such instrument, the Convention shall enter into force on the thirtieth day after the deposit of its own such instrument.

Article 46
Reservations

1. Reservations incompatible with the object and purpose of the present Convention shall not be permitted.
2. Reservations may be withdrawn at any time.

Article 47
Amendments

1. Any State Party may propose an amendment to the present Convention and submit it to the Secretary-General of the United Nations. The Secretary-General shall communicate any proposed amendments to States Parties, with a request to be notified whether they favour a conference of States Parties for the purpose of considering and deciding upon the proposals. In the event that, within four months from the date of such communication, at least one third of the States Parties favour such a conference, the Secretary-General shall convene the conference

under the auspices of the United Nations. Any amendment adopted by a majority of two thirds of the States Parties present and voting shall be submitted by the Secretary-General to the General Assembly for approval and thereafter to all States Parties for acceptance.
2. An amendment adopted and approved in accordance with paragraph 1 of this article shall enter into force on the thirtieth day after the number of instruments of acceptance deposited reaches two thirds of the number of States Parties at the date of adoption of the amendment. Thereafter, the amendment shall enter into force for any State Party on the thirtieth day following the deposit of its own instrument of acceptance. An amendment shall be binding only on those States Parties which have accepted it.
3. If so decided by the Conference of States Parties by consensus, an amendment adopted and approved in accordance with paragraph 1 of this article which relates exclusively to articles 34, 38, 39 and 40 shall enter into force for all States Parties on the thirtieth day after the number of instruments of acceptance deposited reaches two thirds of the number of States Parties at the date of adoption of the amendment.

Article 48
Denunciation

A State Party may denounce the present Convention by written notification to the Secretary-General of the United Nations. The denunciation shall become effective one year after the date of receipt of the notification by the Secretary-General.

Article 49
Accessible format

The text of the present Convention shall be made available in accessible formats.

Article 50
Authentic texts

The Arabic, Chinese, English, French, Russian and Spanish texts of the present Convention shall be equally authentic.

In witness thereof the undersigned plenipotentiaries, being duly authorized thereto by their respective Governments, have signed the present Convention.

Optional Protocol to the Convention on the Rights of Persons with Disabilities (adopted on December 13, 2006, entered into force on May 3, 2008)

The States Parties to the present Protocol have agreed as follows:

Article 1

1. A State Party to the present Protocol ("State Party") recognizes the competence of the Committee on the Rights of Persons with Disabilities ("the Committee") to receive and consider communications from or on behalf of individuals or groups of individuals subject to its jurisdiction who claim to be victims of a violation by that State Party of the provisions of the Convention.
2. No communication shall be received by the Committee if it concerns a State Party to the Convention that is not a party to the present Protocol.

Article 2

The Committee shall consider a communication inadmissible when:

(a) The communication is anonymous;
(b) The communication constitutes an abuse of the right of submission of such communications or is incompatible with the provisions of the Convention;
(c) The same matter has already been examined by the Committee or has been or is being examined under another procedure of international investigation or settlement;
(d) All available domestic remedies have not been exhausted. This shall not be the rule where the application of the remedies is unreasonably prolonged or unlikely to bring effective relief;
(e) It is manifestly ill-founded or not sufficiently substantiated; or when
(f) The facts that are the subject of the communication occurred prior to the entry into force of the present Protocol for the State Party concerned unless those facts continued after that date.

APPENDIX 4

Article 3

Subject to the provisions of article 2 of the present Protocol, the Committee shall bring any communications submitted to it confidentially to the attention of the State Party. Within six months, the receiving State shall submit to the Committee written explanations or statements clarifying the matter and the remedy, if any, that may have been taken by that State.

Article 4

1. At any time after the receipt of a communication and before a determination on the merits has been reached, the Committee may transmit to the State Party concerned for its urgent consideration a request that the State Party take such interim measures as may be necessary to avoid possible irreparable damage to the victim or victims of the alleged violation.
2. Where the Committee exercises its discretion under paragraph 1 of this article, this does not imply a determination on admissibility or on the merits of the communication.

Article 5

The Committee shall hold closed meetings when examining communications under the present Protocol. After examining a communication, the Committee shall forward its suggestions and recommendations, if any, to the State Party concerned and to the petitioner.

Article 6

1. If the Committee receives reliable information indicating grave or systematic violations by a State Party of rights set forth in the Convention, the Committee shall invite that State Party to cooperate in the examination of the information and to this end submit observations with regard to the information concerned.
2. Taking into account any observations that may have been submitted by the State Party concerned as well as any other reliable information available to it, the Committee may designate one or more of its members to conduct an inquiry and to report urgently to the Committee. Where warranted and with the consent of the State Party, the inquiry may include a visit to its territory.
3. After examining the findings of such an inquiry, the Committee shall transmit these findings to the State Party concerned together with any comments and recommendations.

4. The State Party concerned shall, within six months of receiving the findings, comments and recommendations transmitted by the Committee, submit its observations to the Committee.
5. Such an inquiry shall be conducted confidentially and the cooperation of the State Party shall be sought at all stages of the proceedings.

Article 7

1. The Committee may invite the State Party concerned to include in its report under article 35 of the Convention details of any measures taken in response to an inquiry conducted under article 6 of the present Protocol.
2. The Committee may, if necessary, after the end of the period of six months referred to in article 6.4, invite the State Party concerned to inform it of the measures taken in response to such an inquiry.

Article 8

Each State Party may, at the time of signature or ratification of the present Protocol or accession thereto, declare that it does not recognize the competence of the Committee provided for in articles 6 and 7.

Article 9

The Secretary-General of the United Nations shall be the depositary of the present Protocol.

Article 10

The present Protocol shall be open for signature by signatory States and regional integration organizations of the Convention at United Nations Headquarters in New York as of 30 March 2007.

Article 11

The present Protocol shall be subject to ratification by signatory States of this Protocol which have ratified or acceded to the Convention. It shall be subject to formal confirmation by signatory regional integration organizations of this Protocol which have formally confirmed or acceded to the Convention. It shall be open for accession by any State or regional integration organization which has ratified, formally confirmed or acceded to the Convention and which has not signed the Protocol.

Article 12

1. "Regional integration organization" shall mean an organization constituted by sovereign States of a given region, to which its member States have transferred competence in respect of matters governed by the Convention and this Protocol. Such organizations shall declare, in their instruments of formal confirmation or accession, the extent of their competence with respect to matters governed by the Convention and this Protocol. Subsequently, they shall inform the depositary of any substantial modification in the extent of their competence.
2. References to "States Parties" in the present Protocol shall apply to such organizations within the limits of their competence.
3. For the purposes of article 13, paragraph 1, and article 15, paragraph 2, any instrument deposited by a regional integration organization shall not be counted.
4. Regional integration organizations, in matters within their competence, may exercise their right to vote in the meeting of States Parties, with a number of votes equal to the number of their member States that are Parties to this Protocol. Such an organization shall not exercise its right to vote if any of its member States exercises its right, and vice versa.

Article 13

1. Subject to the entry into force of the Convention, the present Protocol shall enter into force on the thirtieth day after the deposit of the tenth instrument of ratification or accession.
2. For each State or regional integration organization ratifying, formally confirming or acceding to the Protocol after the deposit of the tenth such instrument, the Protocol shall enter into force on the thirtieth day after the deposit of its own such instrument.

Article 14

1. Reservations incompatible with the object and purpose of the present Protocol shall not be permitted.
2. Reservations may be withdrawn at any time.

Article 15

1. Any State Party may propose an amendment to the present Protocol and submit it to the Secretary-General of the United Nations. The Secretary-General shall communicate any proposed amendments to States Parties, with a request to be notified whether they favour a meeting of States Parties for the purpose of considering and deciding upon the proposals. In the event that, within four months from the date of such communication, at least one third of the States Parties favour such a meeting, the Secretary-General shall convene the meeting under the auspices of the United Nations. Any amendment adopted by a majority of two thirds of the States Parties present and voting shall be submitted by the Secretary-General to the General Assembly for approval and thereafter to all States Parties for acceptance.
2. An amendment adopted and approved in accordance with paragraph 1 of this article shall enter into force on the thirtieth day after the number of instruments of acceptance deposited reaches two thirds of the number of States Parties at the date of adoption of the amendment. Thereafter, the amendment shall enter into force for any State Party on the thirtieth day following the deposit of its own instrument of acceptance. An amendment shall be binding only on those States Parties which have accepted it.

Article 16

A State Party may denounce the present Protocol by written notification to the Secretary-General of the United Nations. The denunciation shall become effective one year after the date of receipt of the notification by the Secretary-General.

Article 17

The text of the present Protocol shall be made available in accessible formats.

Article 18

The Arabic, Chinese, English, French, Russian and Spanish texts of the present Protocol shall be equally authentic.

In witness thereof the undersigned plenipotentiaries, being duly authorized thereto by their respective Governments, have signed the present Protocol.

APPENDIX 5

Signatories and Contracting Parties to the Convention on the Rights of Persons with Disabilities (as of October 31, 2016)

Participant	Signature	Accession(a) or Ratification
Afghanistan		18 Sep 2012 a
Albania	22 Dec 2009	11 Feb 2013
Algeria	30 Mar 2007	4 Dec 2009
Andorra	27 Apr 2007	11 Mar 2014
Angola		19 May 2014 a
Antigua and Barbuda	30 Mar 2007	7 Jan 2016
Argentina	30 Mar 2007	2 Sep 2008
Armenia	30 Mar 2007	22 Sep 2010
Australia	30 Mar 2007	17 Jul 2008
Austria	30 Mar 2007	26 Sep 2008
Azerbaijan	9 Jan 2008	28 Jan 2009
Bahamas	24 Sep 2013	28 Sep 2015
Bahrain	25 Jun 2007	22 Sep 2011

SIGNATORIES AND CONTRACTING PARTIES TO THE CRPD

Participant	Signature	Accession(a) or Ratification
Bangladesh	9 May 2007	30 Nov 2007
Barbados	19 Jul 2007	27 Feb 2013
Belarus	28 Sep 2015	
Belgium	30 Mar 2007	2 Jul 2009
Belize	9 May 2011	2 Jun 2011
Benin	8 Feb 2008	5 Jul 2012
Bhutan	21 Sep 2010	
Bolivia (Plurinational State of)	13 Aug 2007	16 Nov 2009
Bosnia and Herzegovina	29 Jul 2009	12 Mar 2010
Brazil	30 Mar 2007	1 Aug 2008
Brunei Darussalam	18 Dec 2007	11 Apr 2016
Bulgaria	27 Sep 2007	22 Mar 2012
Burkina Faso	23 May 2007	23 Jul 2009
Burundi	26 Apr 2007	22 May 2014
Cabo Verde	30 Mar 2007	10 Oct 2011
Cambodia	1 Oct 2007	20 Dec 2012
Cameroon	1 Oct 2008	
Canada	30 Mar 2007	11 Mar 2010
Central African Republic	9 May 2007	11 Oct 2016
Chad	26 Sep 2012	
Chile	30 Mar 2007	29 Jul 2008
China	30 Mar 2007	1 Aug 2008
Colombia	30 Mar 2007	10 May 2011
Comoros	26 Sep 2007	16 Jun 2016
Congo	30 Mar 2007	2 Sep 2014

(*Continued*)

APPENDIX 5

Participant	Signature	Accession(a) or Ratification
Cook Islands		8 May 2009 a
Costa Rica	30 Mar 2007	1 Oct 2008
Côte d'Ivoire	7 Jun 2007	10 Jan 2014
Croatia	30 Mar 2007	15 Aug 2007
Cuba	26 Apr 2007	6 Sep 2007
Cyprus	30 Mar 2007	27 Jun 2011
Czech Republic	30 Mar 2007	28 Sep 2009
Democratic People's Republic of Korea	3 Jul 2013	
Democratic Republic of the Congo		30 Sep 2015 a
Denmark	30 Mar 2007	24 Jul 2009
Djibouti		18 Jun 2012 a
Dominica	30 Mar 2007	1 Oct 2012
Dominican Republic	30 Mar 2007	18 Aug 2009
Ecuador	30 Mar 2007	3 Apr 2008
Egypt	4 Apr 2007	14 Apr 2008
El Salvador	30 Mar 2007	14 Dec 2007
Estonia	25 Sep 2007	30 May 2012
Ethiopia	30 Mar 2007	7 Jul 2010
European Union	30 Mar 2007	23 Dec 2010 c
Fiji	2 Jun 2010	
Finland	30 Mar 2007	11 May 2016
France	30 Mar 2007	18 Feb 2010
Gabon	30 Mar 2007	1 Oct 2007
Gambia		6 Jul 2015 a

SIGNATORIES AND CONTRACTING PARTIES TO THE CRPD

Participant	Signature	Accession(a) or Ratification
Georgia	10 Jul 2009	13 Mar 2014
Germany	30 Mar 2007	24 Feb 2009
Ghana	30 Mar 2007	31 Jul 2012
Greece	30 Mar 2007	31 May 2012
Grenada	12 Jul 2010	27 Aug 2014
Guatemala	30 Mar 2007	7 Apr 2009
Guinea	16 May 2007	8 Feb 2008
Guinea-Bissau	24 Sep 2013	24 Sep 2014
Guyana	11 Apr 2007	10 Sep 2014
Haiti		23 Jul 2009 a
Honduras	30 Mar 2007	14 Apr 2008
Hungary	30 Mar 2007	20 Jul 2007
Iceland	30 Mar 2007	23 Sep 2016
India	30 Mar 2007	1 Oct 2007
Indonesia	30 Mar 2007	30 Nov 2011
Iran (Islamic Republic of)		23 Oct 2009 a
Iraq		20 Mar 2013 a
Ireland	30 Mar 2007	
Israel	30 Mar 2007	28 Sep 2012
Italy	30 Mar 2007	15 May 2009
Jamaica	30 Mar 2007	30 Mar 2007
Japan	28 Sep 2007	20 Jan 2014
Jordan	30 Mar 2007	31 Mar 2008
Kazakhstan	11 Dec 2008	21 Apr 2015
Kenya	30 Mar 2007	19 May 2008

(*Continued*)

APPENDIX 5

Participant	Signature	Accession(a) or Ratification
Kiribati		27 Sep 2013 a
Kuwait		22 Aug 2013 a
Kyrgyzstan	21 Sep 2011	
Lao People's Democratic Republic	15 Jan 2008	25 Sep 2009
Latvia	18 Jul 2008	1 Mar 2010
Lebanon	14 Jun 2007	
Lesotho		2 Dec 2008 a
Liberia	30 Mar 2007	26 Jul 2012
Libya	1 May 2008	
Lithuania	30 Mar 2007	18 Aug 2010
Luxembourg	30 Mar 2007	26 Sep 2011
Madagascar	25 Sep 2007	12 Jun 2015
Malawi	27 Sep 2007	27 Aug 2009
Malaysia	8 Apr 2008	19 Jul 2010
Maldives	2 Oct 2007	5 Apr 2010
Mali	15 May 2007	7 Apr 2008
Malta	30 Mar 2007	10 Oct 2012
Marshall Islands		17 Mar 2015 a
Mauritania		3 Apr 2012 a
Mauritius	25 Sep 2007	8 Jan 2010
Mexico	30 Mar 2007	17 Dec 2007
Micronesia (Federated States of)	23 Sep 2011	
Monaco	23 Sep 2009	
Mongolia		13 May 2009 a

SIGNATORIES AND CONTRACTING PARTIES TO THE CRPD

Participant	Signature	Accession(a) or Ratification
Montenegro	27 Sep 2007	2 Nov 2009
Morocco	30 Mar 2007	8 Apr 2009
Mozambique	30 Mar 2007	30 Jan 2012
Myanmar		7 Dec 2011 a
Namibia	25 Apr 2007	4 Dec 2007
Nauru		27 Jun 2012 a
Nepal	3 Jan 2008	7 May 2010
Netherlands	30 Mar 2007	14 Jun 2016
New Zealand	30 Mar 2007	25 Sep 2008
Nicaragua	30 Mar 2007	7 Dec 2007
Niger	30 Mar 2007	24 Jun 2008
Nigeria	30 Mar 2007	24 Sep 2010
Norway	30 Mar 2007	3 Jun 2013
Oman	17 Mar 2008	6 Jan 2009
Pakistan	25 Sep 2008	5 Jul 2011
Palau	20 Sep 2011	11 Jun 2013
Panama	30 Mar 2007	7 Aug 2007
Papua New Guinea	2 Jun 2011	26 Sep 2013
Paraguay	30 Mar 2007	3 Sep 2008
Peru	30 Mar 2007	30 Jan 2008
Philippines	25 Sep 2007	15 Apr 2008
Poland	30 Mar 2007	25 Sep 2012
Portugal	30 Mar 2007	23 Sep 2009
Qatar	9 Jul 2007	13 May 2008
Republic of Korea	30 Mar 2007	11 Dec 2008

(*Continued*)

APPENDIX 5

Participant	Signature	Accession(a) or Ratification
Republic of Moldova	30 Mar 2007	21 Sep 2010
Romania	26 Sep 2007	31 Jan 2011
Russian Federation	24 Sep 2008	25 Sep 2012
Rwanda		15 Dec 2008 a
Samoa	24 Sep 2014	
San Marino	30 Mar 2007	22 Feb 2008
Sao Tome and Principe		5 Nov 2015 a
Saudi Arabia		24 Jun 2008 a
Senegal	25 Apr 2007	7 Sep 2010
Serbia	17 Dec 2007	31 Jul 2009
Seychelles	30 Mar 2007	2 Oct 2009
Sierra Leone	30 Mar 2007	4 Oct 2010
Singapore	30 Nov 2012	18 Jul 2013
Slovakia	26 Sep 2007	26 May 2010
Slovenia	30 Mar 2007	24 Apr 2008
Solomon Islands	23 Sep 2008	
South Africa	30 Mar 2007	30 Nov 2007
Spain	30 Mar 2007	3 Dec 2007
Sri Lanka	30 Mar 2007	8 Feb 2016
St. Lucia	22 Sep 2011	
St. Vincent and the Grenadines		29 Oct 2010 a
State of Palestine		2 Apr 2014 a
Sudan	30 Mar 2007	24 Apr 2009
Suriname	30 Mar 2007	

SIGNATORIES AND CONTRACTING PARTIES TO THE CRPD

Participant	Signature	Accession(a) or Ratification
Swaziland	25 Sep 2007	24 Sep 2012
Sweden	30 Mar 2007	15 Dec 2008
Switzerland		15 Apr 2014 a
Syrian Arab Republic	30 Mar 2007	10 Jul 2009
Thailand	30 Mar 2007	29 Jul 2008
The former Yugoslav Republic of Macedonia	30 Mar 2007	29 Dec 2011
Togo	23 Sep 2008	1 Mar 2011
Tonga	15 Nov 2007	
Trinidad and Tobago	27 Sep 2007	25 Jun 2015
Tunisia	30 Mar 2007	2 Apr 2008
Turkey	30 Mar 2007	28 Sep 2009
Turkmenistan		4 Sep 2008 a
Tuvalu		18 Dec 2013 a
Uganda	30 Mar 2007	25 Sep 2008
Ukraine	24 Sep 2008	4 Feb 2010
United Arab Emirates	8 Feb 2008	19 Mar 2010
United Kingdom of Great Britain and Northern Ireland	30 Mar 2007	8 Jun 2009
United Republic of Tanzania	30 Mar 2007	10 Nov 2009
United States of America	30 Jul 2009	
Uruguay	3 Apr 2007	11 Feb 2009
Uzbekistan	27 Feb 2009	
Vanuatu	17 May 2007	23 Oct 2008
Venezuela (Bolivarian Republic of)		24 Sep 2013 a

(Continued)

APPENDIX 5

Participant	Signature	Accession(a) or Ratification
Viet Nam	22 Oct 2007	5 Feb 2015
Yemen	30 Mar 2007	26 Mar 2009
Zambia	9 May 2008	1 Feb 2010
Zimbabwe		23 Sep 2013 a

APPENDIX 6

Berne Convention for the Protection of Literary and Artistic Works, (Paris Text, as last amended on September 28, 1979)

of September 9, 1886,
completed at PARIS on May 4, 1896,
revised at BERLIN on November 13, 1908,
completed at BERNE on March 20, 1914,
revised at ROME on June 2, 1928,
at BRUSSELS on June 26, 1948,
at STOCKHOLM on July 14, 1967,
and at PARIS on July 24, 1971,
and amended on September 28, 1979

TABLE OF CONTENTS

Article 1:	Establishment of a Union
Article 2:	Protected Works: *1. "Literary and artistic works"; 2. Possible requirement of fixation; 3. Derivative works; 4. Official texts; 5. Collections; 6. Obligation to protect; beneficiaries of protection; 7. Works of applied art and industrial designs; 8. News*
Article 2*bis*:	Possible Limitation of Protection of Certain Works: *1. Certain speeches; 2. Certain uses of lectures and addresses; 3. Right to make collections of such works*
Article 3:	Criteria of Eligibility for Protection: *1. Nationality of author; place of publication of work; 2. Residence*

APPENDIX 6

	of author; 3. "Published" works; 4. "Simultaneously published" works
Article 4:	Criteria of Eligibility for Protection of Cinematographic Works, Works of Architecture and Certain Artistic Works
Article 5:	Rights Guaranteed: *1. and 2. Outside the country of origin; 3. In the country of origin; 4. "Country of origin"*
Article 6:	Possible Restriction of Protection in Respect of Certain Works of Nationals of Certain Countries Outside the Union: *1. In the country of the first publication and in other countries; 2. No retroactivity; 3. Notice*
Article 6*bis*:	Moral Rights: *1. To claim authorship; to object to certain modifications and other derogatory actions; 2. After the author's death; 3. Means of redress*
Article 7:	Term of Protection: *1. Generally; 2. For cinematographic works; 3. For anonymous and pseudonymous works; 4. For photographic works and works of applied art; 5. Starting date of computation; 6. Longer terms; 7. Shorter terms; 8. Applicable law; "comparison" of terms*
Article 7*bis*:	Term of Protection for Works of Joint Authorship
Article 8:	Right of Translation
Article 9:	Right of Reproduction: *1. Generally; 2. Possible exceptions; 3. Sound and visual recordings*
Article 10:	Certain Free Uses of Works: *1. Quotations; 2. Illustrations for teaching; 3. Indication of source and author*
Article 10*bis*:	Further Possible Free Uses of Works: *1. Of certain articles and broadcast works; 2. Of works seen or heard in connection with current events*
Article 11:	Certain Rights in Dramatic and Musical Works: *1. Right of public performance and of communication to the public of a performance; 2. In respect of translations*
Article 11*bis*:	Broadcasting and Related Rights: *1. Broadcasting and other wireless communications, public communication of broadcast by wire or rebroadcast, public communication of broadcast by loudspeaker or analogous instruments; 2. Compulsory licenses; 3. Recording; ephemeral recordings*
Article 11*ter*:	Certain Rights in Literary Works: *1. Right of public recitation and of communication to the public of a recitation; 2. In respect of translations*
Article 12:	Right of Adaptation, Arrangement and Other Alteration
Article 13:	Possible Limitation of the Right of Recording of Musical Works and Any Words Pertaining Thereto: *1. Compulsory licenses; 2. Transitory measures; 3. Seizure on importation of copies made without the author's permission*

Article 14:	Cinematographic and Related Rights: *1. Cinematographic adaptation and reproduction; distribution; public performance and public communication by wire of works thus adapted or reproduced; 2. Adaptation of cinematographic productions; 3. No compulsory licenses*
Article 14bis:	Special Provisions Concerning Cinematographic Works: *1. Assimilation to "original" works; 2. Ownership; limitation of certain rights of certain contributors; 3. Certain other contributors*
Article 14ter:	"Droit de suite" in Works of Art and Manuscripts: *1. Right to an interest in resales; 2. Applicable law; 3. Procedure*
Article 15:	Right to Enforce Protected Rights: *1. Where author's name is indicated or where pseudonym leaves no doubt as to author's identity; 2. In the case of cinematographic works; 3. In the case of anonymous or pseudonymous works; 4. In the case of certain unpublished works of unknown authorship*
Article 16:	Infringing Copies: *1. Seizure; 2. Seizure on importation; 3. Applicable law*
Article 17:	Possibility of Control of Circulation, Presentation and Exhibition of Works
Article 18:	Works Existing on Convention's Entry Into Force: *1. Protectable where protection not yet expired in country of origin; 2. Non-protectable where protection already expired in country where it is claimed; 3. Application of these principles; 4. Special cases*
Article 19:	Protection Greater than Resulting from Convention
Article 20:	Special Agreements Among Countries of the Union
Article 21:	Special Provisions Regarding Developing Countries: *1. Reference to Appendix; 2. Appendix part of Act*
Article 22:	Assembly: *1. Constitution and composition; 2. Tasks; 3. Quorum, voting, observers; 4. Convocation; 5. Rules of procedure*
Article 23:	Executive Committee: *1. Constitution; 2. Composition; 3. Number of members; 4. Geographical distribution; special agreements; 5. Term, limits of re-eligibility, rules of election; 6. Tasks; 7. Convocation; 8. Quorum, voting; 9. Observers; 10. Rules of procedure*
Article 24:	International Bureau: *1. Tasks in general, Director General; 2. General information; 3. Periodical; 4. Information to countries; 5. Studies and services; 6. Participation in meetings; 7. Conferences of revision; 8. Other tasks*
Article 25:	Finances: *1. Budget; 2. Coordination with other Unions; 3. Resources; 4. Contributions; possible extension of previous budget; 5. Fees and charges; 6. Working capital fund; 7. Advances by host Government; 8. Auditing of accounts*

Article 26:	Amendments: *1. Provisions susceptible of amendment by the Assembly; proposals 2. Adoption; 3. Entry into force*
Article 27:	Revision: *1. Objective; 2. Conferences; 3. Adoption*
Article 28:	Acceptance and Entry Into Force of Act for Countries of the Union: *1. Ratification, accession; possibility of excluding certain provisions; withdrawal of exclusion; 2. Entry into force of Articles 1 to 21 and Appendix; 3. Entry into force of Articles 22 to 38*
Article 29:	Acceptance and Entry Into Force for Countries Outside the Union: *1. Accession; 2. Entry into force*
Article 29bis:	Effect of Acceptance of Act for the Purposes of Article 14(2) of the WIPO Convention
Article 30:	Reservations: *1. Limits of possibility of making reservations; 2. Earlier reservations; reservation as to the right of translation; withdrawal of reservation*
Article 31:	Applicability to Certain Territories: *1. Declaration; 2. Withdrawal of declaration; 3. Effective date; 4. Acceptance of factual situations not implied*
Article 32:	Applicability of this Act and of Earlier Acts: *1. As between countries already members of the Union; 2. As between a country becoming a member of the Union and other countries members of the Union; 3. Applicability of the Appendix in Certain Relations*
Article 33:	Disputes: *1. Jurisdiction of the International Court of Justice; 2. Reservation as to such jurisdiction; 3. Withdrawal of reservation*
Article 34:	Closing of Certain Earlier Provisions: *1. Of earlier Acts; 2. Of the Protocol to the Stockholm Act*
Article 35:	Duration of the Convention; Denunciation: *1. Unlimited duration; 2. Possibility of denunciation; 3. Effective date of denunciation; 4. Moratorium on denunciation*
Article 36:	Application of the Convention: *1. Obligation to adopt the necessary measures; 2. Time from which obligation exists*
Article 37:	Final Clauses: *1. Languages of the Act; 2. Signature; 3. Certified copies; 4. Registration; 5. Notifications*
Article 38:	Transitory Provisions: *1. Exercise of the "five-year privilege"; 2. Bureau of the Union, Director of the Bureau; 3. Succession of Bureau of the Union*

APPENDIX
SPECIAL PROVISIONS REGARDING DEVELOPING COUNTRIES

Article I:	Faculties Open to Developing Countries: *1. Availability of certain faculties; declaration; 2. Duration of effect of*

	declaration; 3. Cessation of developing country status; 4. Existing stocks of copies; 5. Declarations concerning certain territories; 6. Limits of reciprocity
Article II:	Limitations on the Right of Translation: *1. Licenses grantable by competent authority; 2 to 4. Conditions allowing the grant of such licenses; 5. Purposes for which licenses may be granted; 6. Termination of licenses; 7. Works composed mainly of illustrations; 8. Works withdrawn from circulation; 9. Licenses for broadcasting organizations*
Article III:	Limitation on the Right of Reproduction: *1. Licenses grantable by competent authority; 2 to 5. Conditions allowing the grant of such licenses; 6. Termination of licenses. 7. Works to which this Article applies*
Article IV:	Provisions Common to Licenses Under Articles II and III: *1 and 2. Procedure; 3. Indication of author and title of work; 4. Exportation of copies; 5. Notice; 6. Compensation*
Article V:	Alternative Possibility for Limitation of the Rights of Translation: *1. Regime provided for under the 1886 and 1896 Acts; 2. No possibility of change to regime under Article II; 3. Time limit for choosing the alternative possibility*
Article VI:	Possibilities of applying, or admitting the application of, certain provisions of the Appendix before becoming bound by it: *1. Declaration; Depository and effective date of declaration*

The countries of the Union, being equally animated by the desire to protect, in as effective and uniform a manner as possible, the rights of authors in their literary and artistic works,

Recognizing the importance of the work of the Revision Conference held at Stockholm in 1967,

Have resolved to revise the Act adopted by the Stockholm Conference, while maintaining without change Articles 1 to 20 and 22 to 26 of that Act.

Consequently, the undersigned Plenipotentiaries, having presented their full powers, recognized as in good and due form, have agreed as follows:

Article 1
Establishment of a Union

The countries to which this Convention applies constitute a Union for the protection of the rights of authors in their literary and artistic works.

Article 2
Protected Works:
1. "Literary and artistic works"; 2. Possible requirement of fixation; 3. Derivative works; 4. Official texts; 5. Collections; 6. Obligation to protect; beneficiaries of protection; 7. Works of applied art and industrial designs; 8. News

(1) The expression "literary and artistic works" shall include every production in the literary, scientific and artistic domain, whatever may be the mode or form of its expression, such as books, pamphlets and other writings; lectures, addresses, sermons and other works of the same nature; dramatic or dramatico-musical works; choreographic works and entertainments in dumb show; musical compositions with or without words; cinematographic works to which are assimilated works expressed by a process analogous to cinematography; works of drawing, painting, architecture, sculpture, engraving and lithography; photographic works to which are assimilated works expressed by a process analogous to photography; works of applied art; illustrations, maps, plans, sketches and three-dimensional works relative to geography, topography, architecture or science.

(2) It shall, however, be a matter for legislation in the countries of the Union to prescribe that works in general or any specified categories of works shall not be protected unless they have been fixed in some material form.

(3) Translations, adaptations, arrangements of music and other alterations of a literary or artistic work shall be protected as original works without prejudice to the copyright in the original work.

(4) It shall be a matter for legislation in the countries of the Union to determine the protection to be granted to official texts of a legislative, administrative and legal nature, and to official translations of such texts.

(5) Collections of literary or artistic works such as encyclopaedias and anthologies which, by reason of the selection and arrangement of their contents, constitute intellectual creations shall be protected as such, without prejudice to the copyright in each of the works forming part of such collections.

(6) The works mentioned in this Article shall enjoy protection in all countries of the Union. This protection shall operate for the benefit of the author and his successors in title.

(7) Subject to the provisions of Article 7(4) of this Convention, it shall be a matter for legislation in the countries of the Union to determine the extent of the application of their laws to works of applied art and industrial designs and models, as well as the conditions under which

such works, designs and models shall be protected. Works protected in the country of origin solely as designs and models shall be entitled in another country of the Union only to such special protection as is granted in that country to designs and models; however, if no such special protection is granted in that country, such works shall be protected as artistic works.

(8) The protection of this Convention shall not apply to news of the day or to miscellaneous facts having the character of mere items of press information.

Article 2bis
Possible Limitation of Protection of Certain Works:
1. Certain speeches; 2. Certain uses of lectures and addresses; 3. Right to make collections of such works

(1) It shall be a matter for legislation in the countries of the Union to exclude, wholly or in part, from the protection provided by the preceding Article political speeches and speeches delivered in the course of legal proceedings.

(2) It shall also be a matter for legislation in the countries of the Union to determine the conditions under which lectures, addresses and other works of the same nature which are delivered in public may be reproduced by the press, broadcast, communicated to the public by wire and made the subject of public communication as envisaged in Article 11bis(1) of this Convention, when such use is justified by the informatory purpose.

(3) Nevertheless, the author shall enjoy the exclusive right of making a collection of his works mentioned in the preceding paragraphs.

Article 3
Criteria of Eligibility for Protection:
1. Nationality of author; place of publication of work; 2. Residence of author; 3. "Published" works; 4. "Simultaneously published" works

(1) The protection of this Convention shall apply to:
   (a) authors who are nationals of one of the countries of the Union, for their works, whether published or not;
   (b) authors who are not nationals of one of the countries of the Union, for their works first published in one of those countries, or simultaneously in a country outside the Union and in a country of the Union.

(2) Authors who are not nationals of one of the countries of the Union but who have their habitual residence in one of them shall, for the purposes of this Convention, be assimilated to nationals of that country.

(3) The expression "published works" means works published with the consent of their authors, whatever may be the means of manufacture of the copies, provided that the availability of such copies has been such as to satisfy the reasonable requirements of the public, having regard to the nature of the work. The performance of a dramatic, dramatico-musical, cinematographic or musical work, the public recitation of a literary work, the communication by wire or the broadcasting of literary or artistic works, the exhibition of a work of art and the construction of a work of architecture shall not constitute publication.

(4) A work shall be considered as having been published simultaneously in several countries if it has been published in two or more countries within thirty days of its first publication.

Article 4
Criteria of Eligibility for Protection of Cinematographic Works, Works of Architecture and Certain Artistic Works

The protection of this Convention shall apply, even if the conditions of Article 3 are not fulfilled, to:

(a) authors of cinematographic works the maker of which has his headquarters or habitual residence in one of the countries of the Union;

(b) authors of works of architecture erected in a country of the Union or of other artistic works incorporated in a building or other structure located in a country of the Union.

Article 5
Rights Guaranteed:
1. and 2. Outside the country of origin; 3. In the country of origin; 4. "Country of origin"

(1) Authors shall enjoy, in respect of works for which they are protected under this Convention, in countries of the Union other than the country of origin, the rights which their respective laws do now or may hereafter grant to their nationals, as well as the rights specially granted by this Convention.

(2) The enjoyment and the exercise of these rights shall not be subject to any formality; such enjoyment and such exercise shall be independent of the existence of protection in the country of origin of the work. Consequently, apart from the provisions of this Convention, the extent of protection, as well as the means of redress afforded to the author to protect his rights, shall be governed exclusively by the laws of the country where protection is claimed.

(3) Protection in the country of origin is governed by domestic law. However, when the author is not a national of the country of origin of the work for which he is protected under this Convention, he shall enjoy in that country the same rights as national authors.

(4) The country of origin shall be considered to be:
   (a) in the case of works first published in a country of the Union, that country; in the case of works published simultaneously in several countries of the Union which grant different terms of protection, the country whose legislation grants the shortest term of protection;
   (b) in the case of works published simultaneously in a country outside the Union and in a country of the Union, the latter country;
   (c) in the case of unpublished works or of works first published in a country outside the Union, without simultaneous publication in a country of the Union, the country of the Union of which the author is a national, provided that:
      (i) when these are cinematographic works the maker of which has his headquarters or his habitual residence in a country of the Union, the country of origin shall be that country, and
      (ii) when these are works of architecture erected in a country of the Union or other artistic works incorporated in a building or other structure located in a country of the Union, the country of origin shall be that country.

Article 6
Possible Restriction of Protection in Respect of Certain Works of Nationals of Certain Countries Outside the Union:
1. In the country of the first publication and in other countries;
2. No retroactivity; 3. Notice

(1) Where any country outside the Union fails to protect in an adequate manner the works of authors who are nationals of one of the countries of the Union, the latter country may restrict the protection given

to the works of authors who are, at the date of the first publication thereof, nationals of the other country and are not habitually resident in one of the countries of the Union. If the country of first publication avails itself of this right, the other countries of the Union shall not be required to grant to works thus subjected to special treatment a wider protection than that granted to them in the country of first publication.

(2) No restrictions introduced by virtue of the preceding paragraph shall affect the rights which an author may have acquired in respect of a work published in a country of the Union before such restrictions were put into force.

(3) The countries of the Union which restrict the grant of copyright in accordance with this Article shall give notice thereof to the Director General of the World Intellectual Property Organization (hereinafter designated as "the Director General") by a written declaration specifying the countries in regard to which protection is restricted, and the restrictions to which rights of authors who are nationals of those countries are subjected. The Director General shall immediately communicate this declaration to all the countries of the Union.

Article 6bis
Moral Rights:
1. To claim authorship; to object to certain modifications and other derogatory actions; 2. After the author's death; 3. Means of redress

(1) Independently of the author's economic rights, and even after the transfer of the said rights, the author shall have the right to claim authorship of the work and to object to any distortion, mutilation or other modification of, or other derogatory action in relation to, the said work, which would be prejudicial to his honor or reputation.

(2) The rights granted to the author in accordance with the preceding paragraph shall, after his death, be maintained, at least until the expiry of the economic rights, and shall be exercisable by the persons or institutions authorized by the legislation of the country where protection is claimed. However, those countries whose legislation, at the moment of their ratification of or accession to this Act, does not provide for the protection after the death of the author of all the rights set out in the preceding paragraph may provide that some of these rights may, after his death, cease to be maintained.

(3) The means of redress for safeguarding the rights granted by this Article shall be governed by the legislation of the country where protection is claimed.

Article 7
Term of Protection:
1. Generally; 2. For cinematographic works; 3. For anonymous and pseudonymous works; 4. For photographic works and works of applied art; 5. Starting date of computation; 6. Longer terms; 7. Shorter terms; 8. Applicable law; "comparison" of terms

(1) The term of protection granted by this Convention shall be the life of the author and fifty years after his death.
(2) However, in the case of cinematographic works, the countries of the Union may provide that the term of protection shall expire fifty years after the work has been made available to the public with the consent of the author, or, failing such an event within fifty years from the making of such a work, fifty years after the making.
(3) In the case of anonymous or pseudonymous works, the term of protection granted by this Convention shall expire fifty years after the work has been lawfully made available to the public. However, when the pseudonym adopted by the author leaves no doubt as to his identity, the term of protection shall be that provided in paragraph (1). If the author of an anonymous or pseudonymous work discloses his identity during the above-mentioned period, the term of protection applicable shall be that provided in paragraph (1). The countries of the Union shall not be required to protect anonymous or pseudonymous works in respect of which it is reasonable to presume that their author has been dead for fifty years.
(4) It shall be a matter for legislation in the countries of the Union to determine the term of protection of photographic works and that of works of applied art in so far as they are protected as artistic works; however, this term shall last at least until the end of a period of twenty-five years from the making of such a work.
(5) The term of protection subsequent to the death of the author and the terms provided by paragraphs (2), (3) and (4) shall run from the date of death or of the event referred to in those paragraphs, but such terms shall always be deemed to begin on the first of January of the year following the death or such event.
(6) The countries of the Union may grant a term of protection in excess of those provided by the preceding paragraphs.

(7) Those countries of the Union bound by the Rome Act of this Convention which grant, in their national legislation in force at the time of signature of the present Act, shorter terms of protection than those provided for in the preceding paragraphs shall have the right to maintain such terms when ratifying or acceding to the present Act.

(8) In any case, the term shall be governed by the legislation of the country where protection is claimed; however, unless the legislation of that country otherwise provides, the term shall not exceed the term fixed in the country of origin of the work.

Article 7bis
Term of Protection for Works of Joint Authorship

The provisions of the preceding Article shall also apply in the case of a work of joint authorship, provided that the terms measured from the death of the author shall be calculated from the death of the last surviving author.

Article 8
Right of Translation

Authors of literary and artistic works protected by this Convention shall enjoy the exclusive right of making and of authorizing the translation of their works throughout the term of protection of their rights in the original works.

Article 9
Right of Reproduction:
1. Generally; 2. Possible exceptions;
3. Sound and visual recordings

(1) Authors of literary and artistic works protected by this Convention shall have the exclusive right of authorizing the reproduction of these works, in any manner or form.

(2) It shall be a matter for legislation in the countries of the Union to permit the reproduction of such works in certain special cases, provided that such reproduction does not conflict with a normal exploitation of the work and does not unreasonably prejudice the legitimate interests of the author.

(3) Any sound or visual recording shall be considered as a reproduction for the purposes of this Convention.

Article 10
Certain Free Uses of Works:
1. Quotations; 2. Illustrations for teaching;
3. Indication of source and author

(1) It shall be permissible to make quotations from a work which has already been lawfully made available to the public, provided that their making is compatible with fair practice, and their extent does not exceed that justified by the purpose, including quotations from newspaper articles and periodicals in the form of press summaries.

(2) It shall be a matter for legislation in the countries of the Union, and for special agreements existing or to be concluded between them, to permit the utilization, to the extent justified by the purpose, of literary or artistic works by way of illustration in publications, broadcasts or sound or visual recordings for teaching, provided such utilization is compatible with fair practice.

(3) Where use is made of works in accordance with the preceding paragraphs of this Article, mention shall be made of the source, and of the name of the author if it appears thereon.

Article 10bis
Further Possible Free Uses of Works:
1. Of certain articles and broadcast works; 2. Of works seen or heard in connection with current events

(1) It shall be a matter for legislation in the countries of the Union to permit the reproduction by the press, the broadcasting or the communication to the public by wire of articles published in newspapers or periodicals on current economic, political or religious topics, and of broadcast works of the same character, in cases in which the reproduction, broadcasting or such communication thereof is not expressly reserved. Nevertheless, the source must always be clearly indicated; the legal consequences of a breach of this obligation shall be determined by the legislation of the country where protection is claimed.

(2) It shall also be a matter for legislation in the countries of the Union to determine the conditions under which, for the purpose of reporting current events by means of photography, cinematography, broadcasting or communication to the public by wire, literary or artistic works seen or heard in the course of the event may, to the extent justified by the informatory purpose, be reproduced and made available to the public.

Article 11
Certain Rights in Dramatic and Musical Works:
1. Right of public performance and of communication to the public of a performance; 2. In respect of translations

(1) Authors of dramatic, dramatico-musical and musical works shall enjoy the exclusive right of authorizing:
   (i) the public performance of their works, including such public performance by any means or process;
   (ii) any communication to the public of the performance of their works.
(2) Authors of dramatic or dramatico-musical works shall enjoy, during the full term of their rights in the original works, the same rights with respect to translations thereof.

Article 11bis
Broadcasting and Related Rights:
1. Broadcasting and other wireless communications, public communication of broadcast by wire or rebroadcast, public communication of broadcast by loudspeaker or analogous instruments; 2. Compulsory licenses; 3. Recording; ephemeral recordings

(1) Authors of literary and artistic works shall enjoy the exclusive right of authorizing:
   (i) the broadcasting of their works or the communication thereof to the public by any other means of wireless diffusion of signs, sounds or images;
   (ii) any communication to the public by wire or by rebroadcasting of the broadcast of the work, when this communication is made by an organization other than the original one;
   (iii) the public communication by loudspeaker or any other analogous instrument transmitting, by signs, sounds or images, the broadcast of the work.
(2) It shall be a matter for legislation in the countries of the Union to determine the conditions under which the rights mentioned in the preceding paragraph may be exercised, but these conditions shall apply only in the countries where they have been prescribed. They shall not in any circumstances be prejudicial to the moral rights of the author, nor to his right to obtain equitable remuneration

which, in the absence of agreement, shall be fixed by competent authority.

(3) In the absence of any contrary stipulation, permission granted in accordance with paragraph (1) of this Article shall not imply permission to record, by means of instruments recording sounds or images, the work broadcast. It shall, however, be a matter for legislation in the countries of the Union to determine the regulations for ephemeral recordings made by a broadcasting organization by means of its own facilities and used for its own broadcasts. The preservation of these recordings in official archives may, on the ground of their exceptional documentary character, be authorized by such legislation.

Article 11ter
Certain Rights in Literary Works:
1. Right of public recitation and of communication to the public of a recitation; 2. In respect of translations

(1) Authors of literary works shall enjoy the exclusive right of authorizing:
   (i) the public recitation of their works, including such public recitation by any means or process;
   (ii) any communication to the public of the recitation of their works.
(2) Authors of literary works shall enjoy, during the full term of their rights in the original works, the same rights with respect to translations thereof.

Article 12
Right of Adaptation, Arrangement and Other Alteration

Authors of literary or artistic works shall enjoy the exclusive right of authorizing adaptations, arrangements and other alterations of their works.

Article 13
Possible Limitation of the Right of Recording of Musical Works and Any Words Pertaining Thereto:
1. Compulsory licenses; 2. Transitory measures; 3. Seizure on importation of copies made without the author's permission

(1) Each country of the Union may impose for itself reservations and conditions on the exclusive right granted to the author of a musical

work and to the author of any words, the recording of which together with the musical work has already been authorized by the latter, to authorize the sound recording of that musical work, together with such words, if any; but all such reservations and conditions shall apply only in the countries which have imposed them and shall not, in any circumstances, be prejudicial to the rights of these authors to obtain equitable remuneration which, in the absence of agreement, shall be fixed by competent authority.

(2) Recordings of musical works made in a country of the Union in accordance with Article 13(3) of the Conventions signed at Rome on June 2, 1928, and at Brussels on June 26, 1948, may be reproduced in that country without the permission of the author of the musical work until a date two years after that country becomes bound by this Act.

(3) Recordings made in accordance with paragraphs (1) and (2) of this Article and imported without permission from the parties concerned into a country where they are treated as infringing recordings shall be liable to seizure.

Article 14
Cinematographic and Related Rights:
1. Cinematographic adaptation and reproduction; distribution; public performance and public communication by wire of works thus adapted or reproduced;
2. Adaptation of cinematographic productions;
3. No compulsory licenses

(1) Authors of literary or artistic works shall have the exclusive right of authorizing:
   (i) the cinematographic adaptation and reproduction of these works, and the distribution of the works thus adapted or reproduced;
   (ii) the public performance and communication to the public by wire of the works thus adapted or reproduced.
(2) The adaptation into any other artistic form of a cinematographic production derived from literary or artistic works shall, without prejudice to the authorization of the author of the cinematographic production, remain subject to the authorization of the authors of the original works.
(3) The provisions of Article 13(1) shall not apply.

Article 14bis
Special Provisions Concerning Cinematographic Works:
1. Assimilation to "original" works; 2. Ownership;
limitation of certain rights of certain contributors;
3. Certain other contributors

(1) Without prejudice to the copyright in any work which may have been adapted or reproduced, a cinematographic work shall be protected as an original work. The owner of copyright in a cinematographic work shall enjoy the same rights as the author of an original work, including the rights referred to in the preceding Article.

(2)
- (a) Ownership of copyright in a cinematographic work shall be a matter for legislation in the country where protection is claimed.
- (b) However, in the countries of the Union which, by legislation, include among the owners of copyright in a cinematographic work authors who have brought contributions to the making of the work, such authors, if they have undertaken to bring such contributions, may not, in the absence of any contrary or special stipulation, object to the reproduction, distribution, public performance, communication to the public by wire, broadcasting or any other communication to the public, or to the subtitling or dubbing of texts, of the work.
- (c) The question whether or not the form of the undertaking referred to above should, for the application of the preceding subparagraph (b), be in a written agreement or a written act of the same effect shall be a matter for the legislation of the country where the maker of the cinematographic work has his headquarters or habitual residence. However, it shall be a matter for the legislation of the country of the Union where protection is claimed to provide that the said undertaking shall be in a written agreement or a written act of the same effect. The countries whose legislation so provides shall notify the Director General by means of a written declaration, which will be immediately communicated by him to all the other countries of the Union.
- (d) By "contrary or special stipulation" is meant any restrictive condition which is relevant to the aforesaid undertaking.

(3) Unless the national legislation provides to the contrary, the provisions of paragraph (2)(b) above shall not be applicable to authors of scenarios, dialogues and musical works created for the making of the

cinematographic work, or to the principal director thereof. However, those countries of the Union whose legislation does not contain rules providing for the application of the said paragraph (2)(b) to such director shall notify the Director General by means of a written declaration, which will be immediately communicated by him to all the other countries of the Union.

Article 14ter
"Droit de suite" in Works of Art and Manuscripts:
1. Right to an interest in resales; 2. Applicable law; 3. Procedure

(1) The author, or after his death the persons or institutions authorized by national legislation, shall, with respect to original works of art and original manuscripts of writers and composers, enjoy the inalienable right to an interest in any sale of the work subsequent to the first transfer by the author of the work.

(2) The protection provided by the preceding paragraph may be claimed in a country of the Union only if legislation in the country to which the author belongs so permits, and to the extent permitted by the country where this protection is claimed.

(3) The procedure for collection and the amounts shall be matters for determination by national legislation.

Article 15
Right to Enforce Protected Rights:
1. Where author's name is indicated or where pseudonym leaves no doubt as to author's identity; 2. In the case of cinematographic works; 3. In the case of anonymous and pseudonymous works; 4. In the case of certain unpublished works of unknown authorship

(1) In order that the author of a literary or artistic work protected by this Convention shall, in the absence of proof to the contrary, be regarded as such, and consequently be entitled to institute infringement proceedings in the countries of the Union, it shall be sufficient for his name to appear on the work in the usual manner. This paragraph shall be applicable even if this name is a pseudonym, where the pseudonym adopted by the author leaves no doubt as to his identity.

(2) The person or body corporate whose name appears on a cinematographic work in the usual manner shall, in the absence of proof to the contrary, be presumed to be the maker of the said work.

(3) In the case of anonymous and pseudonymous works, other than those referred to in paragraph (1) above, the publisher whose name appears on the work shall, in the absence of proof to the contrary, be deemed to represent the author, and in this capacity he shall be entitled to protect and enforce the author's rights. The provisions of this paragraph shall cease to apply when the author reveals his identity and establishes his claim to authorship of the work.

(4)
- *(a)* In the case of unpublished works where the identity of the author is unknown, but where there is every ground to presume that he is a national of a country of the Union, it shall be a matter for legislation in that country to designate the competent authority which shall represent the author and shall be entitled to protect and enforce his rights in the countries of the Union.
- *(b)* Countries of the Union which make such designation under the terms of this provision shall notify the Director General by means of a written declaration giving full information concerning the authority thus designated. The Director General shall at once communicate this declaration to all other countries of the Union.

Article 16
Infringing Copies:
1. Seizure; 2. Seizure on importation; 3. Applicable law

(1) Infringing copies of a work shall be liable to seizure in any country of the Union where the work enjoys legal protection.
(2) The provisions of the preceding paragraph shall also apply to reproductions coming from a country where the work is not protected, or has ceased to be protected.
(3) The seizure shall take place in accordance with the legislation of each country.

Article 17
Possibility of Control of Circulation, Presentation and Exhibition of Works

The provisions of this Convention cannot in any way affect the right of the Government of each country of the Union to permit, to control, or to prohibit, by legislation or regulation, the circulation, presentation, or exhibition of any work or production in regard to which the competent authority may find it necessary to exercise that right.

Article 18
Works Existing on Convention's Entry Into Force:
1. Protectable where protection not yet expired in country of origin; 2. Non-protectable where protection already expired in country where it is claimed; 3. Application of these principles; 4. Special cases

(1) This Convention shall apply to all works which, at the moment of its coming into force, have not yet fallen into the public domain in the country of origin through the expiry of the term of protection.
(2) If, however, through the expiry of the term of protection which was previously granted, a work has fallen into the public domain of the country where protection is claimed, that work shall not be protected anew.
(3) The application of this principle shall be subject to any provisions contained in special conventions to that effect existing or to be concluded between countries of the Union. In the absence of such provisions, the respective countries shall determine, each in so far as it is concerned, the conditions of application of this principle.
(4) The preceding provisions shall also apply in the case of new accessions to the Union and to cases in which protection is extended by the application of Article 7 or by the abandonment of reservations.

Article 19
Protection Greater than Resulting from Convention

The provisions of this Convention shall not preclude the making of a claim to the benefit of any greater protection which may be granted by legislation in a country of the Union.

Article 20
Special Agreements Among Countries of the Union

The Governments of the countries of the Union reserve the right to enter into special agreements among themselves, in so far as such agreements grant to authors more extensive rights than those granted by the Convention, or contain other provisions not contrary to this Convention. The provisions of existing agreements which satisfy these conditions shall remain applicable.

Article 21
Special Provisions Regarding Developing Countries:
1. Reference to Appendix; 2. Appendix part of Act

(1) Special provisions regarding developing countries are included in the Appendix.
(2) Subject to the provisions of Article 28(1)(b), the Appendix forms an integral part of this Act.

Article 22
Assembly:
1. Constitution and composition; 2. Tasks; 3. Quorum, voting, observers; 4. Convocation; 5. Rules of procedure

(1)
  (a) The Union shall have an Assembly consisting of those countries of the Union which are bound by Articles 22 to 26.
  (b) The Government of each country shall be represented by one delegate, who may be assisted by alternate delegates, advisors, and experts.
  (c) The expenses of each delegation shall be borne by the Government which has appointed it.

(2)
  (a) The Assembly shall:
    (i) deal with all matters concerning the maintenance and development of the Union and the implementation of this Convention;
    (ii) give directions concerning the preparation for conferences of revision to the International Bureau of Intellectual Property (hereinafter designated as "the International Bureau") referred to in the Convention Establishing the World Intellectual Property Organization (hereinafter designated as "the Organization"), due account being taken of any comments made by those countries of the Union which are not bound by Articles 22 to 26;
    (iii) review and approve the reports and activities of the Director General of the Organization concerning the Union, and give him all necessary instructions concerning matters within the competence of the Union;

(iv) elect the members of the Executive Committee of the Assembly;
(v) review and approve the reports and activities of its Executive Committee, and give instructions to such Committee;
(vi) determine the program and adopt the biennial budget of the Union, and approve its final accounts;
(vii) adopt the financial regulations of the Union;
(viii) establish such committees of experts and working groups as may be necessary for the work of the Union;
(ix) determine which countries not members of the Union and which intergovernmental and international non-governmental organizations shall be admitted to its meetings as observers;
(x) adopt amendments to Articles 22 to 26;
(xi) take any other appropriate action designed to further the objectives of the Union;
(xii) exercise such other functions as are appropriate under this Convention;
(xiii) subject to its acceptance, exercise such rights as are given to it in the Convention establishing the Organization.

(b) With respect to matters which are of interest also to other Unions administered by the Organization, the Assembly shall make its decisions after having heard the advice of the Coordination Committee of the Organization.

(3)
(a) Each country member of the Assembly shall have one vote.
(b) One-half of the countries members of the Assembly shall constitute a quorum.
(c) Notwithstanding the provisions of subparagraph (b), if, in any session, the number of countries represented is less than one-half but equal to or more than one-third of the countries members of the Assembly, the Assembly may make decisions but, with the exception of decisions concerning its own procedure, all such decisions shall take effect only if the following conditions are fulfilled. The International Bureau shall communicate the said decisions to the countries members of the Assembly which were not represented and shall invite them to express in writing their vote or abstention within a period of three months from the date of the communication. If, at the expiration of this period, the number of countries having thus expressed their vote or abstention attains the number of countries which was lacking for attaining the quorum in the session itself, such decisions shall take effect provided that at the same time the required majority still obtains.

(d) Subject to the provisions of Article 26(2), the decisions of the Assembly shall require two-thirds of the votes cast.
(e) Abstentions shall not be considered as votes.
(f) A delegate may represent, and vote in the name of, one country only.
(g) Countries of the Union not members of the Assembly shall be admitted to its meetings as observers.

(4)
(a) The Assembly shall meet once in every second calendar year in ordinary session upon convocation by the Director General and, in the absence of exceptional circumstances, during the same period and at the same place as the General Assembly of the Organization.
(b) The Assembly shall meet in extraordinary session upon convocation by the Director General, at the request of the Executive Committee or at the request of one-fourth of the countries members of the Assembly.

(5) The Assembly shall adopt its own rules of procedure.

Article 23
Executive Committee:
1. Constitution; 2. Composition; 3. Number of members; 4. Geographical distribution; special agreements; 5. Term, limits of re-eligibility, rules of election; 6. Tasks; 7. Convocation; 8. Quorum, voting; 9. Observers; 10. Rules of procedure

(1) The Assembly shall have an Executive Committee.

(2)
(a) The Executive Committee shall consist of countries elected by the Assembly from among countries members of the Assembly. Furthermore, the country on whose territory the Organization has its headquarters shall, subject to the provisions of Article 25(7)(b), have an ex officio seat on the Committee.
(b) The Government of each country member of the Executive Committee shall be represented by one delegate, who may be assisted by alternate delegates, advisors, and experts.
(c) The expenses of each delegation shall be borne by the Government which has appointed it.

(3) The number of countries members of the Executive Committee shall correspond to one-fourth of the number of countries members of the Assembly. In establishing the number of seats to be filled, remainders after division by four shall be disregarded.

(4) In electing the members of the Executive Committee, the Assembly shall have due regard to an equitable geographical distribution and to the need for countries party to the Special Agreements which might be established in relation with the Union to be among the countries constituting the Executive Committee.

(5)
- (a) Each member of the Executive Committee shall serve from the close of the session of the Assembly which elected it to the close of the next ordinary session of the Assembly.
- (b) Members of the Executive Committee may be re-elected, but not more than two-thirds of them.
- (c) The Assembly shall establish the details of the rules governing the election and possible re-election of the members of the Executive Committee.

(6)
- (a) The Executive Committee shall:
  - (i) prepare the draft agenda of the Assembly;
  - (ii) submit proposals to the Assembly respecting the draft program and biennial budget of the Union prepared by the Director General;
  - (iii) [*deleted*]
  - (iv) submit, with appropriate comments, to the Assembly the periodical reports of the Director General and the yearly audit reports on the accounts;
  - (v) in accordance with the decisions of the Assembly and having regard to circumstances arising between two ordinary sessions of the Assembly, take all necessary measures to ensure the execution of the program of the Union by the Director General;
  - (vi) perform such other functions as are allocated to it under this Convention.
- (b) With respect to matters which are of interest also to other Unions administered by the Organization, the Executive Committee shall make its decisions after having heard the advice of the Coordination Committee of the Organization.

(7)
- (a) The Executive Committee shall meet once a year in ordinary session upon convocation by the Director General, preferably during the same period and at the same place as the Coordination Committee of the Organization.
- (b) The Executive Committee shall meet in extraordinary session upon convocation by the Director General, either on his own initiative, or at the request of its Chairman or one-fourth of its members.

(8)
- (a) Each country member of the Executive Committee shall have one vote.
- (b) One-half of the members of the Executive Committee shall constitute a quorum.
- (c) Decisions shall be made by a simple majority of the votes cast.
- (d) Abstentions shall not be considered as votes.
- (e) A delegate may represent, and vote in the name of, one country only.

(9) Countries of the Union not members of the Executive Committee shall be admitted to its meetings as observers.

(10) The Executive Committee shall adopt its own rules of procedure.

Article 24
International Bureau:
1. Tasks in general, Director General; 2. General information; 3. Periodical; 4. Information to countries; 5. Studies and services; 6. Participation in meetings; 7. Conferences of revision; 8. Other tasks

(1)
- (a) The administrative tasks with respect to the Union shall be performed by the International Bureau, which is a continuation of the Bureau of the Union united with the Bureau of the Union established by the International Convention for the Protection of Industrial Property.
- (b) In particular, the International Bureau shall provide the secretariat of the various organs of the Union.
- (c) The Director General of the Organization shall be the chief executive of the Union and shall represent the Union.

(2) The International Bureau shall assemble and publish information concerning the protection of copyright. Each country of the Union shall promptly communicate to the International Bureau all new laws and official texts concerning the protection of copyright.

(3) The International Bureau shall publish a monthly periodical.

(4) The International Bureau shall, on request, furnish information to any country of the Union on matters concerning the protection of copyright.

(5) The International Bureau shall conduct studies, and shall provide services, designed to facilitate the protection of copyright.

(6) The Director General and any staff member designated by him shall participate, without the right to vote, in all meetings of the Assembly,

the Executive Committee and any other committee of experts or working group. The Director General, or a staff member designated by him, shall be ex officio secretary of these bodies.

(7)
- (a) The International Bureau shall, in accordance with the directions of the Assembly and in cooperation with the Executive Committee, make the preparations for the conferences of revision of the provisions of the Convention other than Articles 22 to 26.
- (b) The International Bureau may consult with intergovernmental and international non-governmental organizations concerning preparations for conferences of revision.
- (c) The Director General and persons designated by him shall take part, without the right to vote, in the discussions at these conferences.

(8) The International Bureau shall carry out any other tasks assigned to it.

Article 25
Finances:
1. Budget; 2. Coordination with other Unions; 3. Resources;
4. Contributions; possible extension of previous budget; 5. Fees and charges; 6. Working capital fund; 7. Advances by host Government;
8. Auditing of accounts

(1)
- (a) The Union shall have a budget.
- (b) The budget of the Union shall include the income and expenses proper to the Union, its contribution to the budget of expenses common to the Unions, and, where applicable, the sum made available to the budget of the Conference of the Organization.
- (c) Expenses not attributable exclusively to the Union but also to one or more other Unions administered by the Organization shall be considered as expenses common to the Unions. The share of the Union in such common expenses shall be in proportion to the interest the Union has in them.

(2) The budget of the Union shall be established with due regard to the requirements of coordination with the budgets of the other Unions administered by the Organization.

(3) The budget of the Union shall be financed from the following sources:
- (i) contributions of the countries of the Union;
- (ii) fees and charges due for services performed by the International Bureau in relation to the Union;

(iii) sale of, or royalties on, the publications of the International Bureau concerning the Union;
(iv) gifts, bequests, and subventions;
(v) rents, interests, and other miscellaneous income.

(4)
(a) For the purpose of establishing its contribution towards the budget, each country of the Union shall belong to a class, and shall pay its annual contributions on the basis of a number of units fixed as follows:

Class I 25
Class II 20
Class III 15
Class IV 10
Class V 5
Class VI 3
Class VII 1

(b) Unless it has already done so, each country shall indicate, concurrently with depositing its instrument of ratification or accession, the class to which it wishes to belong. Any country may change class. If it chooses a lower class, the country must announce it to the Assembly at one of its ordinary sessions. Any such change shall take effect at the beginning of the calendar year following the session.

(c) The annual contribution of each country shall be an amount in the same proportion to the total sum to be contributed to the annual budget of the Union by all countries as the number of its units is to the total of the units of all contributing countries.

(d) Contributions shall become due on the first of January of each year.

(e) A country which is in arrears in the payment of its contributions shall have no vote in any of the organs of the Union of which it is a member if the amount of its arrears equals or exceeds the amount of the contributions due from it for the preceding two full years. However, any organ of the Union may allow such a country to continue to exercise its vote in that organ if, and as long as, it is satisfied that the delay in payment is due to exceptional and unavoidable circumstances.

(f) If the budget is not adopted before the beginning of a new financial period, it shall be at the same level as the budget of the previous year, in accordance with the financial regulations.

(5) The amount of the fees and charges due for services rendered by the International Bureau in relation to the Union shall be established, and shall be reported to the Assembly and the Executive Committee, by the Director General.

(6)
- (a) The Union shall have a working capital fund which shall be constituted by a single payment made by each country of the Union. If the fund becomes insufficient, an increase shall be decided by the Assembly.
- (b) The amount of the initial payment of each country to the said fund or of its participation in the increase thereof shall be a proportion of the contribution of that country for the year in which the fund is established or the increase decided.
- (c) The proportion and the terms of payment shall be fixed by the Assembly on the proposal of the Director General and after it has heard the advice of the Coordination Committee of the Organization.

(7)
- (a) In the headquarters agreement concluded with the country on the territory of which the Organization has its headquarters, it shall be provided that, whenever the working capital fund is insufficient, such country shall grant advances. The amount of these advances and the conditions on which they are granted shall be the subject of separate agreements, in each case, between such country and the Organization. As long as it remains under the obligation to grant advances, such country shall have an ex officio seat on the Executive Committee.
- (b) The country referred to in subparagraph (a) and the Organization shall each have the right to denounce the obligation to grant advances, by written notification. Denunciation shall take effect three years after the end of the year in which it has been notified.

(8) The auditing of the accounts shall be effected by one or more of the countries of the Union or by external auditors, as provided in the financial regulations. They shall be designated, with their agreement, by the Assembly.

Article 26
Amendments:

1. Provisions susceptible of amendment by the Assembly; proposals; 2. Adoption; 3. Entry into force

(1) Proposals for the amendment of Articles 22, 23, 24, 25, and the present Article, may be initiated by any country member of the Assembly, by the Executive Committee, or by the Director General. Such proposals shall be communicated by the Director General to the member

countries of the Assembly at least six months in advance of their consideration by the Assembly.
(2) Amendments to the Articles referred to in paragraph (1) shall be adopted by the Assembly. Adoption shall require three-fourths of the votes cast, provided that any amendment of Article 22, and of the present paragraph, shall require four-fifths of the votes cast.
(3) Any amendment to the Articles referred to in paragraph (1) shall enter into force one month after written notifications of acceptance, effected in accordance with their respective constitutional processes, have been received by the Director General from three-fourths of the countries members of the Assembly at the time it adopted the amendment. Any amendment to the said Articles thus accepted shall bind all the countries which are members of the Assembly at the time the amendment enters into force, or which become members thereof at a subsequent date, provided that any amendment increasing the financial obligations of countries of the Union shall bind only those countries which have notified their acceptance of such amendment.

Article 27
Revision:
1. Objective; 2. Conferences; 3. Adoption

(1) This Convention shall be submitted to revision with a view to the introduction of amendments designed to improve the system of the Union.
(2) For this purpose, conferences shall be held successively in one of the countries of the Union among the delegates of the said countries.
(3) Subject to the provisions of Article 26 which apply to the amendment of Articles 22 to 26, any revision of this Act, including the Appendix, shall require the unanimity of the votes cast.

Article 28
Acceptance and Entry Into Force of Act for Countries of the Union:
1. Ratification, accession; possibility of excluding certain provisions; withdrawal of exclusion; 2. Entry into force of Articles 1 to 21 and Appendix; 3. Entry into force of Articles 22 to 38

(1)
(a) Any country of the Union which has signed this Act may ratify it, and, if it has not signed it, may accede to it. Instruments of ratification or accession shall be deposited with the Director General.

(b) Any country of the Union may declare in its instrument of ratification or accession that its ratification or accession shall not apply to Articles 1 to 21 and the Appendix, provided that, if such country has previously made a declaration under Article VI(1) of the Appendix, then it may declare in the said instrument only that its ratification or accession shall not apply to Articles 1 to 20.

(c) Any country of the Union which, in accordance with subparagraph (b), has excluded provisions therein referred to from the effects of its ratification or accession may at any later time declare that it extends the effects of its ratification or accession to those provisions. Such declaration shall be deposited with the Director General.

(2)
(a) Articles 1 to 21 and the Appendix shall enter into force three months after both of the following two conditions are fulfilled:
  (i) at least five countries of the Union have ratified or acceded to this Act without making a declaration under paragraph (1)(b),
  (ii) France, Spain, the United Kingdom of Great Britain and Northern Ireland, and the United States of America, have become bound by the Universal Copyright Convention as revised at Paris on July 24, 1971.

(b) The entry into force referred to in subparagraph (a) shall apply to those countries of the Union which, at least three months before the said entry into force, have deposited instruments of ratification or accession not containing a declaration under paragraph (1)(b).

(c) With respect to any country of the Union not covered by subparagraph (b) and which ratifies or accedes to this Act without making a declaration under paragraph (1)(b), Articles 1 to 21 and the Appendix shall enter into force three months after the date on which the Director General has notified the deposit of the relevant instrument of ratification or accession, unless a subsequent date has been indicated in the instrument deposited. In the latter case, Articles 1 to 21 and the Appendix shall enter into force with respect to that country on the date thus indicated.

(d) The provisions of subparagraphs (a) to (c) do not affect the application of Article VI of the Appendix.

(3) With respect to any country of the Union which ratifies or accedes to this Act with or without a declaration made under paragraph (1)(b), Articles 22 to 38 shall enter into force three months after the date on which the Director General has notified the deposit of the relevant instrument of ratification or accession, unless a subsequent date has been indicated in the instrument deposited. In the latter case, Articles 22 to 38 shall enter into force with respect to that country on the date thus indicated.

Article 29
Acceptance and Entry Into Force for Countries Outside the Union:
1. Accession; 2. Entry into force

(1) Any country outside the Union may accede to this Act and thereby become party to this Convention and a member of the Union. Instruments of accession shall be deposited with the Director General.

(2)
   (a) Subject to subparagraph (b), this Convention shall enter into force with respect to any country outside the Union three months after the date on which the Director General has notified the deposit of its instrument of accession, unless a subsequent date has been indicated in the instrument deposited. In the latter case, this Convention shall enter into force with respect to that country on the date thus indicated.

   (b) If the entry into force according to subparagraph (a) precedes the entry into force of Articles 1 to 21 and the Appendix according to Article 28(2)(a), the said country shall, in the meantime, be bound, instead of by Articles 1 to 21 and the Appendix, by Articles 1 to 20 of the Brussels Act of this Convention.

Article 29bis
Effect of Acceptance of Act for the Purposes of Article 14(2) of the WIPO Convention

Ratification of or accession to this Act by any country not bound by Articles 22 to of the Stockholm Act of this Convention shall, for the sole purposes of Article 14(2) of the Convention establishing the Organization, amount to ratification of or accession to the said Stockholm Act with the limitation set forth in Article 28(1)(b)(i) thereof.

Article 30
Reservations:
1. Limits of possibility of making reservations;
2. Earlier reservations; reservation as to the right of translation; withdrawal of reservation

(1) Subject to the exceptions permitted by paragraph (2) of this Article, by Article 28(1)(b), by Article 33(2), and by the Appendix, ratification or accession shall automatically entail acceptance of all the provisions and admission to all the advantages of this Convention.

(2)

    (a) Any country of the Union ratifying or acceding to this Act may, subject to Article V(2) of the Appendix, retain the benefit of the reservations it has previously formulated on condition that it makes a declaration to that effect at the time of the deposit of its instrument of ratification or accession.

    (b) Any country outside the Union may declare, in acceding to this Convention and subject to Article V(2) of the Appendix, that it intends to substitute, temporarily at least, for Article 8 of this Act concerning the right of translation, the provisions of Article 5 of the Union Convention of 1886, as completed at Paris in 1896, on the clear understanding that the said provisions are applicable only to translations into a language in general use in the said country. Subject to Article I(6)(b) of the Appendix, any country has the right to apply, in relation to the right of translation of works whose country of origin is a country availing itself of such a reservation, a protection which is equivalent to the protection granted by the latter country.

    (c) Any country may withdraw such reservations at any time by notification addressed to the Director General.

Article 31
Applicability to Certain Territories:
1. Declaration; 2. Withdrawal of declaration; 3. Effective date;
4. Acceptance of factual situations not implied

(1) Any country may declare in its instrument of ratification or accession, or may inform the Director General by written notification at any time thereafter, that this Convention shall be applicable to all or part of those territories, designated in the declaration or notification, for the external relations of which it is responsible.

(2) Any country which has made such a declaration or given such a notification may, at any time, notify the Director General that this Convention shall cease to be applicable to all or part of such territories.

(3)

    (a) Any declaration made under paragraph (1) shall take effect on the same date as the ratification or accession in which it was included, and any notification given under that paragraph shall take effect three months after its notification by the Director General.

    (b) Any notification given under paragraph (2) shall take effect twelve months after its receipt by the Director General.

(4) This Article shall in no way be understood as implying the recognition or tacit acceptance by a country of the Union of the factual situation concerning a territory to which this Convention is made applicable

Article 32
Applicability of this Act and of Earlier Acts:
1. As between countries already members of the Union; 2. As between a country becoming a member of the Union and other countries members of the Union; 3. Applicability of the Appendix in Certain Relations

(1) This Act shall, as regards relations between the countries of the Union, and to the extent that it applies, replace the Berne Convention of September 9, 1886, and the subsequent Acts of revision. The Acts previously in force shall continue to be applicable, in their entirety or to the extent that this Act does not replace them by virtue of the preceding sentence, in relations with countries of the Union which do not ratify or accede to this Act.

(2) Countries outside the Union which become party to this Act shall, subject to paragraph (3), apply it with respect to any country of the Union not bound by this Act or which, although bound by this Act, has made a declaration pursuant to Article 28(1)(b). Such countries recognize that the said country of the Union, in its relations with them:
   (i) may apply the provisions of the most recent Act by which it is bound, and
   (ii) subject to Article I(6) of the Appendix, has the right to adapt the protection to the level provided for by this Act.

(3) Any country which has availed itself of any of the faculties provided for in the Appendix may apply the provisions of the Appendix relating to the faculty or faculties of which it has availed itself in its relations with any other country of the Union which is not bound by this Act, provided that the latter country has accepted the application of the said provisions.

Article 33
Disputes:
1. Jurisdiction of the International Court of Justice; 2. Reservation as to such jurisdiction; 3. Withdrawal of reservation

(1) Any dispute between two or more countries of the Union concerning the interpretation or application of this Convention, not settled by negotiation, may, by any one of the countries concerned, be brought before the International Court of Justice by application in conformity with the Statute of the Court, unless the countries concerned agree on some other method of settlement. The country bringing

the dispute before the Court shall inform the International Bureau; the International Bureau shall bring the matter to the attention of the other countries of the Union.
(2) Each country may, at the time it signs this Act or deposits its instrument of ratification or accession, declare that it does not consider itself bound by the provisions of paragraph (1). With regard to any dispute between such country and any other country of the Union, the provisions of paragraph (1) shall not apply.
(3) Any country having made a declaration in accordance with the provisions of paragraph (2) may, at any time, withdraw its declaration by notification addressed to the Director General.

Article 34
Closing of Certain Earlier Provisions:
1. Of earlier Acts; 2. Of the Protocol to the Stockholm Act

(1) Subject to Article 29*bis*, no country may ratify or accede to earlier Acts of this Convention once Articles 1 to 21 and the Appendix have entered into force.
(2) Once Articles 1 to 21 and the Appendix have entered into force, no country may make a declaration under Article 5 of the Protocol Regarding Developing Countries attached to the Stockholm Act.

Article 35
Duration of the Convention; Denunciation:
1. Unlimited duration; 2. Possibility of denunciation;
3. Effective date of denunciation; 4. Moratorium on denunciation

(1) This Convention shall remain in force without limitation as to time.
(2) Any country may denounce this Act by notification addressed to the Director General. Such denunciation shall constitute also denunciation of all earlier Acts and shall affect only the country making it, the Convention remaining in full force and effect as regards the other countries of the Union.
(3) Denunciation shall take effect one year after the day on which the Director General has received the notification.
(4) The right of denunciation provided by this Article shall not be exercised by any country before the expiration of five years from the date upon which it becomes a member of the Union.

Article 36
Application of the Convention:
1. Obligation to adopt the necessary measures;
2. Time from which obligation exists

(1) Any country party to this Convention undertakes to adopt, in accordance with its constitution, the measures necessary to ensure the application of this Convention.

(2) It is understood that, at the time a country becomes bound by this Convention, it will be in a position under its domestic law to give effect to the provisions of this Convention.

Article 37
Final Clauses:
1. Languages of the Act; 2. Signature; 3. Certified copies; 4. Registration; 5. Notifications

(1)
  (a) This Act shall be signed in a single copy in the French and English languages and, subject to paragraph (2), shall be deposited with the Director General.
  (b) Official texts shall be established by the Director General, after consultation with the interested Governments, in the Arabic, German, Italian, Portuguese and Spanish languages, and such other languages as the Assembly may designate.
  (c) In case of differences of opinion on the interpretation of the various texts, the French text shall prevail.

(2) This Act shall remain open for signature until January 31, 1972. Until that date, the copy referred to in paragraph (1)(a) shall be deposited with the Government of the French Republic.

(3) The Director General shall certify and transmit two copies of the signed text of this Act to the Governments of all countries of the Union and, on request, to the Government of any other country.

(4) The Director General shall register this Act with the Secretariat of the United Nations.

(5) The Director General shall notify the Governments of all countries of the Union of signatures, deposits of instruments of ratification or accession and any declarations included in such instruments or made pursuant to Articles 28(1)(c), 30(2)(a) and (b), and 33(2), entry into force of any provisions of this Act, notifications of denunciation, and notifications pursuant to Articles 30(2)(c), 31(1) and (2), 33(3), and 38(1), as well as the Appendix.

Article 38
Transitory Provisions:
1. Exercise of the "five-year privilege"; 2. Bureau of the Union, Director of the Bureau; 3. Succession of Bureau of the Union

(1) Countries of the Union which have not ratified or acceded to this Act and which are not bound by Articles 22 to 26 of the Stockholm Act of this Convention may, until April 26, 1975, exercise, if they so desire, the rights provided under the said Articles as if they were bound by them. Any country desiring to exercise such rights shall give written notification to this effect to the Director General; this notification shall be effective on the date of its receipt. Such countries shall be deemed to be members of the Assembly until the said date.

(2) As long as all the countries of the Union have not become Members of the Organization, the International Bureau of the Organization shall also function as the Bureau of the Union, and the Director General as the Director of the said Bureau.

(3) Once all the countries of the Union have become Members of the Organization, the rights, obligations, and property, of the Bureau of the Union shall devolve on the International Bureau of the Organization.

APPENDIX
SPECIAL PROVISIONS REGARDING DEVELOPING COUNTRIES

Article I
Faculties Open to Developing Countries:
1. Availability of certain faculties; declaration; 2. Duration of effect of declaration; 3. Cessation of developing country status; 4. Existing stocks of copies; 5. Declarations concerning certain territories; 6. Limits of reciprocity

(1) Any country regarded as a developing country in conformity with the established practice of the General Assembly of the United Nations which ratifies or accedes to this Act, of which this Appendix forms an integral part, and which, having regard to its economic situation and its social or cultural needs, does not consider itself immediately in a position to make provision for the protection of all the rights as provided for in this Act, may, by a notification deposited with the Director General at the time of depositing its instrument of ratification or accession or, subject to Article V(1)(c), at any time thereafter, declare that it will avail itself of the faculty provided for in Article II, or

of the faculty provided for in Article III, or of both of those faculties. It may, instead of availing itself of the faculty provided for in Article II, make a declaration according to Article V(1)(a).

(2)
- (a) Any declaration under paragraph (1) notified before the expiration of the period of ten years from the entry into force of Articles 1 to 21 and this Appendix according to Article 28(2) shall be effective until the expiration of the said period. Any such declaration may be renewed in whole or in part for periods of ten years each by a notification deposited with the Director General not more than fifteen months and not less than three months before the expiration of the ten-year period then running.
- (b) Any declaration under paragraph (1) notified after the expiration of the period of ten years from the entry into force of Articles 1 to 21 and this Appendix according to Article 28(2) shall be effective until the expiration of the ten-year period then running. Any such declaration may be renewed as provided for in the second sentence of subparagraph (a).

(3) Any country of the Union which has ceased to be regarded as a developing country as referred to in paragraph (1) shall no longer be entitled to renew its declaration as provided in paragraph (2), and, whether or not it formally withdraws its declaration, such country shall be precluded from availing itself of the faculties referred to in paragraph (1) from the expiration of the ten-year period then running or from the expiration of a period of three years after it has ceased to be regarded as a developing country, whichever period expires later.

(4) Where, at the time when the declaration made under paragraph (1) or (2) ceases to be effective, there are copies in stock which were made under a license granted by virtue of this Appendix, such copies may continue to be distributed until their stock is exhausted.

(5) Any country which is bound by the provisions of this Act and which has deposited a declaration or a notification in accordance with Article 31(1) with respect to the application of this Act to a particular territory, the situation of which can be regarded as analogous to that of the countries referred to in paragraph (1), may, in respect of such territory, make the declaration referred to in paragraph (1) and the notification of renewal referred to in paragraph (2). As long as such declaration or notification remains in effect, the provisions of this Appendix shall be applicable to the territory in respect of which it was made.

(6)
- (a) The fact that a country avails itself of any of the faculties referred to in paragraph (1) does not permit another country to give less

protection to works of which the country of origin is the former country than it is obliged to grant under Articles 1 to 20.

(b) The right to apply reciprocal treatment provided for in Article 30(2)(b), second sentence, shall not, until the date on which the period applicable under Article I(3) expires, be exercised in respect of works the country of origin of which is a country which has made a declaration according to Article V(1)(a).

Article II
Limitations on the Right of Translation:

1. Licenses grantable by competent authority; 2. to 4. Conditions allowing the grant of such licenses; 5. Purposes for which licenses may be granted; 6. Termination of licenses; 7. Works composed mainly of illustrations; 8. Works withdrawn from circulation; 9. Licenses for broadcasting organizations

(1) Any country which has declared that it will avail itself of the faculty provided for in this Article shall be entitled, so far as works published in printed or analogous forms of reproduction are concerned, to substitute for the exclusive right of translation provided for in Article 8 a system of non-exclusive and non-transferable licenses, granted by the competent authority under the following conditions and subject to Article IV.

(2)
 (a) Subject to paragraph (3), if, after the expiration of a period of three years, or of any longer period determined by the national legislation of the said country, commencing on the date of the first publication of the work, a translation of such work has not been published in a language in general use in that country by the owner of the right of translation, or with his authorization, any national of such country may obtain a license to make a translation of the work in the said language and publish the translation in printed or analogous forms of reproduction.
 (b) A license under the conditions provided for in this Article may also be granted if all the editions of the translation published in the language concerned are out of print.

(3)
 (a) In the case of translations into a language which is not in general use in one or more developed countries which are members of the Union, a period of one year shall be substituted for the period of three years referred to in paragraph (2)(a).

(b) Any country referred to in paragraph (1) may, with the unanimous agreement of the developed countries which are members of the Union and in which the same language is in general use, substitute, in the case of translations into that language, for the period of three years referred to in paragraph (2)(a) a shorter period as determined by such agreement but not less than one year. However, the provisions of the foregoing sentence shall not apply where the language in question is English, French or Spanish. The Director General shall be notified of any such agreement by the Governments which have concluded it.

(4)
(a) No license obtainable after three years shall be granted under this Article until a further period of six months has elapsed, and no license obtainable after one year shall be granted under this Article until a further period of nine months has elapsed

   (i) from the date on which the applicant complies with the requirements mentioned in Article IV(1), or
   (ii) where the identity or the address of the owner of the right of translation is unknown, from the date on which the applicant sends, as provided for in Article IV(2), copies of his application submitted to the authority competent to grant the license.

(b) If, during the said period of six or nine months, a translation in the language in respect of which the application was made is published by the owner of the right of translation or with his authorization, no license under this Article shall be granted.

(5) Any license under this Article shall be granted only for the purpose of teaching, scholarship or research.

(6) If a translation of a work is published by the owner of the right of translation or with his authorization at a price reasonably related to that normally charged in the country for comparable works, any license granted under this Article shall terminate if such translation is in the same language and with substantially the same content as the translation published under the license. Any copies already made before the license terminates may continue to be distributed until their stock is exhausted.

(7) For works which are composed mainly of illustrations, a license to make and publish a translation of the text and to reproduce and publish the illustrations may be granted only if the conditions of Article III are also fulfilled.

(8) No license shall be granted under this Article when the author has withdrawn from circulation all copies of his work.

(9)
- (*a*) A license to make a translation of a work which has been published in printed or analogous forms of reproduction may also be granted to any broadcasting organization having its headquarters in a country referred to in paragraph (1), upon an application made to the competent authority of that country by the said organization, provided that all of the following conditions are met:
    - (i) the translation is made from a copy made and acquired in accordance with the laws of the said country;
    - (ii) the translation is only for use in broadcasts intended exclusively for teaching or for the dissemination of the results of specialized technical or scientific research to experts in a particular profession;
    - (iii) the translation is used exclusively for the purposes referred to in condition (ii) through broadcasts made lawfully and intended for recipients on the territory of the said country, including broadcasts made through the medium of sound or visual recordings lawfully and exclusively made for the purpose of such broadcasts;
    - (iv) all uses made of the translation are without any commercial purpose.
- (*b*) Sound or visual recordings of a translation which was made by a broadcasting organization under a license granted by virtue of this paragraph may, for the purposes and subject to the conditions referred to in subparagraph (a) and with the agreement of that organization, also be used by any other broadcasting organization having its headquarters in the country whose competent authority granted the license in question.
- (*c*) Provided that all of the criteria and conditions set out in subparagraph (a) are met, a license may also be granted to a broadcasting organization to translate any text incorporated in an audio-visual fixation where such fixation was itself prepared and published for the sole purpose of being used in connection with systematic instructional activities.
- (*d*) Subject to subparagraphs (a) to (c), the provisions of the preceding paragraphs shall apply to the grant and exercise of any license granted under this paragraph.

Article III
Limitation on the Right of Reproduction:
1. Licenses grantable by competent authority; 2. to 5. Conditions allowing the grant of such licenses; 6. Termination of licenses; 7. Works to which this Article applies

(1) Any country which has declared that it will avail itself of the faculty provided for in this Article shall be entitled to substitute for the exclusive right of reproduction provided for in Article 9 a system of non-exclusive and non-transferable licenses, granted by the competent authority under the following conditions and subject to Article IV.

(2)
- (a) If, in relation to a work to which this Article applies by virtue of paragraph (7), after the expiration of
  - (i) the relevant period specified in paragraph (3), commencing on the date of first publication of a particular edition of the work, or
  - (ii) any longer period determined by national legislation of the country referred to in paragraph (1), commencing on the same date, copies of such edition have not been distributed in that country to the general public or in connection with systematic instructional activities, by the owner of the right of reproduction or with his authorization, at a price reasonably related to that normally charged in the country for comparable works, any national of such country may obtain a license to reproduce and publish such edition at that or a lower price for use in connection with systematic instructional activities.
- (b) A license to reproduce and publish an edition which has been distributed as described in subparagraph (a) may also be granted under the conditions provided for in this Article if, after the expiration of the applicable period, no authorized copies of that edition have been on sale for a period of six months in the country concerned to the general public or in connection with systematic instructional activities at a price reasonably related to that normally charged in the country for comparable works.

(3) The period referred to in paragraph (2)(a)(i) shall be five years, except that
- (i) for works of the natural and physical sciences, including mathematics, and of technology, the period shall be three years;
- (ii) for works of fiction, poetry, drama and music, and for art books, the period shall be seven years.

APPENDIX 6

(4)
  (a) No license obtainable after three years shall be granted under this Article until a period of six months has elapsed
      (i) from the date on which the applicant complies with the requirements mentioned in Article IV(1), or
      (ii) where the identity or the address of the owner of the right of reproduction is unknown, from the date on which the applicant sends, as provided for in Article IV(2), copies of his application submitted to the authority competent to grant the license.
  (b) Where licenses are obtainable after other periods and Article IV(2) is applicable, no license shall be granted until a period of three months has elapsed from the date of the dispatch of the copies of the application.
  (c) If, during the period of six or three months referred to in subparagraphs (a) and (b), a distribution as described in paragraph (2)(a) has taken place, no license shall be granted under this Article.
  (d) No license shall be granted if the author has withdrawn from circulation all copies of the edition for the reproduction and publication of which the license has been applied for.
(5) A license to reproduce and publish a translation of a work shall not be granted under this Article in the following cases:
    (i) where the translation was not published by the owner of the right of translation or with his authorization, or
    (ii) where the translation is not in a language in general use in the country in which the license is applied for.
(6) If copies of an edition of a work are distributed in the country referred to in paragraph (1) to the general public or in connection with systematic instructional activities, by the owner of the right of reproduction or with his authorization, at a price reasonably related to that normally charged in the country for comparable works, any license granted under this Article shall terminate if such edition is in the same language and with substantially the same content as the edition which was published under the said license. Any copies already made before the license terminates may continue to be distributed until their stock is exhausted.
(7)
  (a) Subject to subparagraph (b), the works to which this Article applies shall be limited to works published in printed or analogous forms of reproduction.

(b) This Article shall also apply to the reproduction in audio-visual form of lawfully made audio-visual fixations including any protected works incorporated therein and to the translation of any incorporated text into a language in general use in the country in which the license is applied for, always provided that the audio-visual fixations in question were prepared and published for the sole purpose of being used in connection with systematic instructional activities.

Article IV
Provisions Common to Licenses Under Articles II and III:
1. and 2. Procedure; 3. Indication of author and title of work; 4. Exportation of copies; 5. Notice; 6. Compensation

(1) A license under Article II or Article III may be granted only if the applicant, in accordance with the procedure of the country concerned, establishes either that he has requested, and has been denied, authorization by the owner of the right to make and publish the translation or to reproduce and publish the edition, as the case may be, or that, after due diligence on his part, he was unable to find the owner of the right. At the same time as making the request, the applicant shall inform any national or international information center referred to in paragraph (2).

(2) If the owner of the right cannot be found, the applicant for a license shall send, by registered airmail, copies of his application, submitted to the authority competent to grant the license, to the publisher whose name appears on the work and to any national or international information center which may have been designated, in a notification to that effect deposited with the Director General, by the Government of the country in which the publisher is believed to have his principal place of business.

(3) The name of the author shall be indicated on all copies of the translation or reproduction published under a license granted under Article II or Article III. The title of the work shall appear on all such copies. In the case of a translation, the original title of the work shall appear in any case on all the said copies.

(4)
  (a) No license granted under Article II or Article III shall extend to the export of copies, and any such license shall be valid only for

publication of the translation or of the reproduction, as the case may be, in the territory of the country in which it has been applied for.

(b) For the purposes of subparagraph (a), the notion of export shall include the sending of copies from any territory to the country which, in respect of that territory, has made a declaration under Article I(5).

(c) Where a governmental or other public entity of a country which has granted a license to make a translation under Article II into a language other than English, French or Spanish sends copies of a translation published under such license to another country, such sending of copies shall not, for the purposes of subparagraph (a), be considered to constitute export if all of the following conditions are met:

    (i) the recipients are individuals who are nationals of the country whose competent authority has granted the license, or organizations grouping such individuals;

    (ii) the copies are to be used only for the purpose of teaching, scholarship or research;

    (iii) the sending of the copies and their subsequent distribution to recipients is without any commercial purpose; and

    (iv) the country to which the copies have been sent has agreed with the country whose competent authority has granted the license to allow the receipt, or distribution, or both, and the Director General has been notified of the agreement by the Government of the country in which the license has been granted.

(5) All copies published under a license granted by virtue of Article II or Article III shall bear a notice in the appropriate language stating that the copies are available for distribution only in the country or territory to which the said license applies.

(6)

(a) Due provision shall be made at the national level to ensure

    (i) that the license provides, in favour of the owner of the right of translation or of reproduction, as the case may be, for just compensation that is consistent with standards of royalties normally operating on licenses freely negotiated between persons in the two countries concerned, and

    (ii) payment and transmittal of the compensation: should national currency regulations intervene, the competent authority shall make all efforts, by the use of international machinery, to ensure transmittal in internationally convertible currency or its equivalent.

(b) Due provision shall be made by national legislation to ensure a correct translation of the work, or an accurate reproduction of the particular edition, as the case may be.

Article V
Alternative Possibility for Limitation of the Right of Translation:
1. Regime provided for under the 1886 and 1896 Acts;
2. No possibility of change to regime under Article II;
3. Time limit for choosing the alternative possibility

(1)
    (a) Any country entitled to make a declaration that it will avail itself of the faculty provided for in Article II may, instead, at the time of ratifying or acceding to this Act:
        (i) if it is a country to which Article 30(2)(a) applies, make a declaration under that provision as far as the right of translation is concerned;
        (ii) if it is a country to which Article 30(2)(a) does not apply, and even if it is not a country outside the Union, make a declaration as provided for in Article 30(2)(b), first sentence.
    (b) In the case of a country which ceases to be regarded as a developing country as referred to in Article I(1), a declaration made according to this paragraph shall be effective until the date on which the period applicable under Article I(3) expires.
    (c) Any country which has made a declaration according to this paragraph may not subsequently avail itself of the faculty provided for in Article II even if it withdraws the said declaration.

(2) Subject to paragraph (3), any country which has availed itself of the faculty provided for in Article II may not subsequently make a declaration according to paragraph (1).

(3) Any country which has ceased to be regarded as a developing country as referred to in Article I(1) may, not later than two years prior to the expiration of the period applicable under Article I(3), make a declaration to the effect provided for in Article 30(2)(b), first sentence, notwithstanding the fact that it is not a country outside the Union. Such declaration shall take effect at the date on which the period applicable under Article I(3) expires.

APPENDIX 6

Article VI
Possibilities of applying, or admitting the application of, certain provisions of the Appendix before becoming bound by it:
1. Declaration; 2. Depository and effective date of declaration

(1) Any country of the Union may declare, as from the date of this Act, and at any time before becoming bound by Articles 1 to 21 and this Appendix:
  (i) if it is a country which, were it bound by Articles 1 to 21 and this Appendix, would be entitled to avail itself of the faculties referred to in Article I(1), that it will apply the provisions of Article II or of Article III or of both to works whose country of origin is a country which, pursuant to (ii) below, admits the application of those Articles to such works, or which is bound by Articles 1 to 21 and this Appendix; such declaration may, instead of referring to Article II, refer to Article V;
  (ii) that it admits the application of this Appendix to works of which it is the country of origin by countries which have made a declaration under (i) above or a notification under Article I.
(2) Any declaration made under paragraph (1) shall be in writing and shall be deposited with the Director General. The declaration shall become effective from the date of its deposit.

INDEX

Agreement on Trade-Related Aspects of Intellectual Property Rights (TRIPS), 5, 7–8, 46, 67–69
   Article 7, 7
   Article 8, 7
Argentina, xv, xvii
audiobook, xxii, 22–24, 41–42, 47–48
Australia, xvii, 84, 87
Austria, 35, 37, 84
authorized entities, 24–31, 44–45
Authors Guild, Inc. v. HathiTrust, 28, 76

beneficiary persons, 14, 23–25, 27, 29–30, 31–38, 41–42, 45, 47–48, 55–57, 61, 72–73, 82–83
   caregivers for, 25, 40, 45
   consultation with, xx, xxv, 19–20, 83
   definition of, 31–38
   direct exchanges between, 61
   exports by, 53–55
   safe harbors for, 45–46, 56–57
   TPMs and, 62–67
blindness, 32–37, 69–79
Berne Convention. *See* Berne Convention for the Protection of Literary and Artistic Works
Berne Convention for the Protection of Literary and Artistic Works, 5, 22, 41–42, 47, 52, 58, 67–69, 71–73

1967 Stockholm Revision to the Berne Convention, 68–69, 72
   Article 2(1), 22
   Article 6*bis*, 42
   Article 9(2), 67–68, 71
book famine, xxi–xxii, 47
Braille, xv, 7, 24, 36, 41, 43, 48

Canada, xvii, 33
Chafee Amendment to the 1976 U.S. Copyright Act, 28, 76
commercial availability, xix, xiv, 47–49, 55, 60, 71, 73, 77
Convention on the Rights of Persons with Disabilities (CRPD), xvi, xxi–xxii, 1, 3, 8–10, 12–13, 15–20, 32, 38, 50, 63, 65, 73, 76, 78–80, 83–84, 86–87
   Article 1, 16–18
   Article 4, 18–19
   Article 5, 18
   Article 9, 9, 17–18
   Article 21, 17
   Article 24, 9, 17
   Article 30, 1, 9, 13, 17–18, 73
   Article 33, 19, 79
   coordination point, 79–80
   focal point, 79–80
   Optional Protocol to, 16, 86

INDEX

Committee on the Rights of Persons with Disabilities, xvi, 3–4, 9, 15–19, 86–87
   General Comment No. 2, 9, 17–19, 87
   General Comment No. 4, 9, 87
Council of Europe, 9
CRPD. *See* Convention on the Rights of Persons with Disabilities

developing countries, xxi, 17, 31, 34–35

e-book, xxii, 23–24, 42, 48, 65
E&Ls. *See* exceptions and limitations to copyright
European Convention on Human Rights, 6, 14
European Union (EU), 9–10, 37, 65
   Information Society Directive, 9–10, 37
exceptions and limitations to copyright, 20–21, 23, 31, 38–51, 58–60, 62, 67–74, 78
   disability-related, 36–38
   EU InfoSoc Directive and, 9, 37, 65
   fair dealing, xix, 8, 46
   fair use, xix, 8, 46, 61, 76
   remuneration, xix, xxiv, 41, 49–51, 60, 72–73
   TST and, 38, 44–46, 56, 58–60, 67–74
exhaustion of rights, 53, 59–61

General Comments. *See also* Committee on the Rights of Persons with Disabilities, 3, 9, 15, 17, 18–19, 86–88

India, xvii, 33, 37
Indonesia, 36–37
International Covenant on Civil and Political Rights (ICCPR), 3, 17
International Covenant on Economic, Social and Cultural Rights (ICESCR), 3, 6–7, 17
Israel, xvii, 37, 57

least-developed countries, 46–47, 61

Marrakesh Treaty to Facilitate Access to Published Works for Persons Who Are Blind, Visually Impaired, or Otherwise Print Disabled (Marrakesh Treaty, MT or Treaty)
   Article 2(a), 21–23, 72
   Article 2(b), 23–24, 37, 65

Article 2(c), 24–31, 52, 57
Article 3, 31–38
Article 4, xix, 25, 38–51, 55–56, 59–60, 62–63, 72–73
Article 5, xix, 39, 49, 51–60, 62, 67
Article 6, 39, 51–53, 55–56, 60–62
Article 7, 39, 62–67
Article 8, 26, 82
Article 10, 58, 75
Article 11, 38, 44, 46, 58, 67, 71
Article 13, 81
Assembly of Contracting Parties, 81
Preamble, xix, 1, 13, 15, 71, 91
Marrakesh Treaty—Agreed Statements, 12, 22, 24, 27–28, 30, 34, 47, 55, 57, 59–60, 66, 73
   Agreed Statement to Article 2(a), 22, 24
   Agreed Statement to Article 2(c), 30
   Agreed Statement to Article 3(b), 34
   Agreed Statement to Article 4(3), 47
   Agreed Statement to Article 4(4), 73
   Agreed Statement to Article 5(1), 55
   Agreed Statement to Article 5(2), 57
   Agreed Statement to Article 5(4), 59
   Agreed Statement to Article 6, 60
   Agreed Statement to Article 7, 66
   Agreed Statement to Article 9, 27–28

national human rights institutions (NHRIs), 75–76, 78–79, 83

Office of the High Commissioner for Human Rights (OHCHR), 88

perceptual disability, xvii, 32–36

reading disability, xvii, 32–36
remuneration. *See also* exceptions and limitations to copyright, xix, xxiv, 41, 49–51, 60, 72

safe harbor, xix, xxiii, 43–47, 56–57, 59, 68, 70–71
sui generis, 46–47, 57–59

INDEX

technological protection measures (TPMs), 39, 62–67, 77, 84
three-step test (TST), xix, xxiii, 38, 44–46, 56, 58–60, 67–74
treaty interpretation, xxiv, 1–2, 11–15, 54–55, 71, 73, 91
TRIPS Agreement or TRIPS. *See* Agreement on Trade-Related Aspects of Intellectual Property Rights

United Nations, xvi, xx–xxi, xxv, 1–5, 7, 15, 85–86, 88–89
UN General Assembly, 2, 16
UN Charter, 88
UN Convention on the Rights of Persons with Disabilities. *See* Convention on the Rights of Persons with Disabilities (CRPD)
UN Committee on the Rights of Persons with Disabilities. *See* Committee on the Rights of Persons with Disabilities
UN Human Rights Council, 86, 88–89
UN Special Rapporteur in the Field of Cultural Rights, 7, 9, 50, 74
UN Special Rapporteur on the Rights of Persons with Disabilities, 89

U.S. Copyright Office, 64
U.S. Library of Congress, 64–65, 80
Universal Declaration of Human Rights (UDHR), 1–3, 13, 15, 91
Universal Periodic Review (UPR), 88

Vienna Convention on the Law of Treaties (VCLT), 11–12
Visual disability/impairment, xv, xvii, 7, 10, 13, 32–36, 38

WIPO Copyright Treaty (WCT), 39, 53, 58–59, 62, 64, 67–68, 71–72
  Article 10, 71–72
  Article 10 Agreed Statement, 71–72
WIPO Performances and Phonograms Treaty (WPPT), 62, 64
World Blind Union, xxii, 28
World Intellectual Property Organization (WIPO), xvii, 4–5, 40, 62, 70, 91
  1967 Convention Establishing the World Intellectual Property Organization, 4
World Trade Organization (WTO), 5, 8, 45
  Dispute Settlement Body, 5